A GUIDE TO MUSIC PERCEPTION

Do You Hear What I Hear?

A GUIDE TO MUSIC PERCEPTION

Do You Hear What I Hear?

RONALD J. SHERROD
Music Department
University of Texas at Tyler

Chris-Lo Publishing Company

Chris-Lo Publishing Company

ISBN 13: 978-1534739161
ISBN 10: 1534739165

To Lonna, with love

TABLE OF CONTENTS

PART II: HISTORICAL PERSPECTIVES

Preface

DO YOU HEAR WHAT I HEAR?: *A Guide to Music Perception* is designed for college and university introductory music appreciation classes of one semester in length. The material covered is organized into twelve chapters under two divisions.

Part *I* of this book. *Foundations for Listening,* Introduces the elements of music and musical instruments. It is the belief of this author that by experiencing musical components on a small scale, listening tools are developed that can be applied when more complicated compositions are encountered. Therefore, folk songs (hopefully familiar to the majority of students), visual diagrams, and suggested physical movements are utilized. The use of examples written in conventional music notation has been intentionally avoided.

Part *II, Historical Perspectives,* paints a picture of the musical heritage of Western culture with a rather broad brush. The traditional divisions into style periods are outlined but the wider view of gradual changes and the non-musical events leading to those changes are also given attention.

Each chapter of the book concludes with the presentation of a renown composer and a representative composition. It is almost universally agreed that these twelve have made the most profound contributions to the development of music. Their biographies are presented, however, not solely from a musical standpoint, but from the position that these composers were people of seriousness, humor, intellect, education, deep feelings, and strong convictions.

I gratefully acknowledge the valuable assistance of Vlcki Samson for her research of the composers' biographies and Susan Murray for her expertise in typesetting and book layout. I extend my appreciation to my wife, Martha, my son, Chris, and to my daughter, Lonna, for their helpful review and comments, but mostly for their love.

Ronald J. Sherrod

PART I

FOUNDATIONS FOR LISTENING

Chapter 1

INTRODUCTION

WHAT IS MUSIC?

Music As a Language

Just as a spoken language is a form of communication, so is music. But, while speech relies on exact parallels between words and real objects, music communicates with the human spirit through other means. While some music, called **program music** does try to tell a story or paint a specific picture, often a composer will rely on the manipulation of sounds to produce emotions and feelings that cannot be produced by other means. Do these emotions have names like love, despair, anger, etc.? Not exactly, because even those abstract concepts are always transformed by the mind into real people, places, or situations. (Try thinking of "friendship" without a person popping into your mind.) Music that conveys feelings and meaning without the need for words or images is call **absolute music**. This is the type of communication that Felix Mendelssohn was referring to when he said,

> *So much is written about music, yet so little is really said. I firmly believe that words are insufficient to describe music, and if I found that they did suffice, I would not need to make music any longer."*

But, music *is* similar to language in some interesting ways. Just as in order to speak a language one must have command of vocabulary, grammar, and syntax, these elements exist in communicating through sound. To say that music is a universal language is not true. A person could probably travel from the United States to a remote village in Madagascar and, through hand signals and facial expressions, transmit and receive elemental information, but the person would not be speaking Malagasy. Similarly, the attraction of sounds coming from an instrument might draw people of different cultures together for a brief period of time due to curiosity. But to truly receive the message intended by the music, a person must not only be familiar with the music's formational elements such as scales, rhythmic cycles, tonal tendencies, and formal design, but the person must also be acutely sensitive to the music's role in its given society. (You may be saying to yourself right now, "I enjoy music, but I'm not familiar with those things." Response: Yes, you are. You may not have names and labels for those elements, but you have been learning them since before you were born.) Thus, the **Ramayana chants** of Bali carry tremendous emotional importance for the people of that country, but (unfortunately) might make a person from California laugh. The people are simply speaking different musical languages.

Music is also often a form of communication in regards to status in society. Many examples could be cited. The songs of the **Noh dramas** of Japan were only intended to be heard by the royalty. In parts of Tanzania there are some songs and dances to be performed only by the women of the society, and there are some strictly for the males. In the United States music distinguishes groups and sub-groups, and makes value judgments about those groups. An individual attending a symphony concert might be looked upon by an uneducated person as pretentious. High school students attending a rock concert dress the same and bob up and down together in a display of conformity specific to that age group. The modern-day listener to a type of music called "contemporary adult jazz" is often a person who owns fine clothes and a nice car, who is beginning the climb up the corporate ladder, and who is careful to be politically correct. Statements about social status are also made when the music of certain groups is *not* given attention. For example, country-western music and gospel music, two of the most widely listened to types of music in the United States, are seldom mentioned in college textbooks.

Music Reflects Our Humanity

It is recognized that the human exists on three levels. The first is the level of basic instincts. On this level we find ourselves as animals, searching for food and protection, and exhibiting selfishness, fear, and rage. The second level separates humankind from the animals. We can look at the past and look into the future. This allows us to formulate plans, learn from trial and error, test a hypothesis, and form an opinion. From this ability we are able to solve mathematical problems, identify geometric designs, use logic, and seek solutions that are "reasonable." Also on this level we can understand another's point of view. But people know that they are more than what is expressed in either of the two above-mentioned levels. Humans seek purpose in life, have knowledge of moral absolutes, search for the answers to questions about existence, God, and ultimate destiny. We know that we are more than mere flesh and blood. On this level we have the ability to truly love (not just naming the reasons why you "logically" love someone) and to truly forgive. On this level a person will fight, even to the point of sacrificing life itself, for what the person believes.

Music reflects and speaks to each of these three levels. On the first level are sounds in nature, wind undulating in a bamboo shoot, taut strings vibrating when plucked, and the regular beat created by the pulsations of the heart within the human body. People then take the sounds and, through logic and reasoning, combine them into compositions that have shape, patterns, unity and contrast. Knowledge of materials and understanding acoustics permit instruments to be built that are resonant and mathematically in tune. The human can detect in music the balance between tension and release that the person seeks in everyday living. Also, on this second level, a very unique thing occurs: The human recognizes the necessity of the human factor in the definition of music. For example, the singing of birds or the sound of waves breaking on a beach is not usually considered music, but a composition written to imitate birds or the sound of the ocean *is* music. But, on the third level, the wonder of the affect of music on the soul causes the listener to ponder such deeper questions of how the mind works, when did it all start, and why am I moved by the music. The three levels were summed up by John Adams, the second President of the United States, in a letter to his wife Abigail.

I must study politics and war, that my sons may have liberty to study mathematics and philosophy. My sons ought to study mathematics and philosophy, geography, natural history, navigation, commerce and agriculture in order to give their children a right to study painting, poetry, music, architecture, statuary, tapestry, and porcelain.

LISTENING TO MUSIC

Types Of Listeners

In our society we are surrounded by music. Music has always been used to enhance joy, sadness, love, rage, serenity, worship, work, and play, but only in very recent years do we find ourselves surrounded by music in department stores, supermarkets, offices, and factories. Movies and television shows would be dull without music, and compact discs and Walkmans are a normal part of our daily lives. What used to be a special event — the hearing of music — has become commonplace. This means that we often "hear" music but seldom "listen to" music. This is not to say that the only purpose of music is for concentration and analysis. In fact, the contrary is probably true in the overall scope of things, but another dimension is added to a person's life if skill is developed in recognizing musical elements and styles. In order to put this in perspective, let us look at various types of listeners.

One type of listener is the **passive listener**. This person is really not a listener at all but is the "hearer" mentioned above. The person uses music as a background for other activities. An example might be the person who comes home from work, turns on the stereo system, sits down, and reads the evening paper. At any given moment the person probably could not tell you what song was being played. Though not listening directly to the music, the passive listener can create desired feelings and mood changes by selecting appropriate music. Or, the passive listener may be unconsciously influenced by music, as in the dentist's chair, Italian restaurant, or Sears.

Another type of listener is the person who uses music for the purpose of relating to other events or situations. The music may remind the person of the ocean, the mountains, trees,

7

rain, or a far away place. The music might bring to mind an experience from the past that can be relived again. This type of listener could be described as the **associative listener**. The person is aware of the music and may be moved by it at a wedding, dance, or political rally.

A third type of listener is the **analytical listener**. This person probably has had some degree of music training or has taken a college level music listening class and can discuss the details of rhythm, melody, harmony, instrumental technique, and historical performance practices. Generally, most people are least aware of the analytical level of listening. Highly trained musicians, orchestra conductors, and choir directors may sometimes seem to operate on this level to the point of dullness or boredom. But, the truth of the matter is that the majority of these people see music with such depth that they fully understand the value of continually broadening their knowledge of all components of music in order to have tools with which to reflect upon human potential and some of the astounding accomplishments of mankind as exemplified in the works of the famous composers.

So, how should one listen to music? Should it be to "not listen" as with the passive listener, to listen very subjectively as with the associative listener, or to be totally objective as with the analytical listener? The answer is to listen to music on all levels, depending on situations and moods. At times one would approach these three planes independently. At other times one would listen on different levels simultaneously. The important thing is to develop a variety of skills in order to have the ability to listen and discuss music as desired. The famous American composer Aaron Copland gave us a valuable image when he wrote:

> *In a sense, the ideal listener is both inside and outside the music at the same moment, judging it and enjoying it, wishing it would go one way and watching it go*

another — almost like the composer at the moment he composes it, because in order to write his music, the composer must also be inside and outside his music, carried away by it and yet coldly critical of it.

What To Listen For

"Carried away by it." That's the emotional impact of the music. "Coldly critical of it." That's the *ways and means* of creating the emotional impact. The more a person is able to aurally recognize the ways and means, the more likely it is that the person will be emotionally affected. While the remainder of this book focuses on numerous specific aspects of music and listening, there are many details that can immediately be drawn to one's attention.

Melody. Most music has a prominent melody. What instrument is playing the melody? Does the melody consist of long smooth sounds or short disconnected sounds? Is the melody plain or do you detect the use of vibrato (sometimes this can be detected visually before it is noticed aurally)? Are there little decorations like trills and grace notes added to the melody? Does only one instrument carry the melody all the way through or do other instruments share the responsibility?

Performing Medium. What specific type of group are you listening to? Is it a brass ensemble or a string quartet? Is it a symphony orchestra or concert band? Is one music instrument being featured as soloist? If you are listening to a choir, is it singing a cappella or with instrumental accompaniment? If you are listening to vocal music, does the expression of the music correspond to the message of the words?

Does the performing medium stay constantly at one volume level or does it use wide ranges of loud and soft?

Clarity. Listen for the clarity of the music. Musicians in a group *could* choose to play independent of the ensemble, but they usually try to blend. This produces clarity. At the same time, each section of an orchestra (strings, woodwinds, brass, percussion), for example, are often meant to be distinguished from the others. Are solos clearly heard apart from the entire ensemble? If words are being sung, these should be clear and easy to understand.

Rhythm. Take notice of the speed of the music. Is it fast or slow? Is the beat of the music strong and accented or is a musical pulse missing altogether? Does the music speed up or slow down? Is there a repetitive rhythmic pattern that is distinctive?

Form. Attempt to grasp a concept of the overall structure of the musical composition. The structure of the music should be solid. When an architect designs a house, the house should look good. The walls should be straight, the fixtures should be functional, and the colors should be complementary. Within this framework, it is possible to design countless numbers of houses, none of which is exactly identical to the other. So it is with music. No two music compositions are the same, but every one should be supported by sound structural design. Whether speaking of an architect or a composer, if a designer chooses to vary from normal expectations, that person must be able to give a defense for the changes. The defense must meet the rigors of reason and logic.

Craftsmanship. Just as the carpenter who builds the house designed by the architect must master tools in order to cut straight lines, accurately use a tape measure, carve out a beautiful fireplace mantel or stair banister, etc., so must musicians be able to control the instruments they play. This means, among other things, the playing of clear musical tones, the smooth connection or the distinct separation of these tones, the ability to play the tones fast or slow, the control over loudness or softness, and the command over phrasing and expression.

Thus, you can be more closely drawn to the music if you are aware of the above factors of music. The more factors presented simultaneously, the more of a challenge for you, but, at the same time, the more rewarding result. Going back to the architect, it is like comparing the designing of a house with the designing of a huge building. Does this mean you will like the music? Not necessarily. Does it mean you will understand the music? Yes. Does it mean that you will be able to discern highly developed skills from rudimentary skills? Yes. Does it mean that you will gain a greater appreciation for the higher developed skills? Yes.

Listening Composition

FOUR SEASONS, *Spring*, 1st mvt.
Baroque Style Period

ANTONIO VIVALDI
1678-1741

Born in Venice, Italy, Antonio Vivaldi was the son of a leading violinist at St. Mark's Cathedral. He studied music with his father while he prepared for the priesthood. Vivaldi played and taught violin, conducted, and until a year before his death (when he moved to Vienna) held a permanent appointment as chief administrator of the Musical Seminary of the Pieta, where orphaned and illegitimate girls were sheltered and taught music.

Many of Vivaldi's works were written for special concerts and festivals at the Pieta, and were performed by the girls who lived there. The musical abilities of the girls were famous; the orchestra was considered one of the best in Italy.

Vivaldi was ordained a priest while he was still a young man, but poor health caused him to serve actively for only one year. He was accused of leaving mass to write music. But Vivaldi responded to these charges as follows:

I have not said mass for 25 years, and I will never say it again, not because of any official order, but by my own will, because of an illness that I have had since birth and which still causes me trouble. After I was ordained priest, I said mass for a little over a year, and then

*stopped, because three times I had to leave the altar
before the end of the service due to my illness. I nearly
always remain indoors for this reason, never going out
except in a gondola or a carriage, because I have difficulty walking due to the pain in my chest. No one asks
me to go to his house, not even our prince, since everyone
is aware of my weakness. I am able to go out after dinner
but not on foot. This is the reason I do not say mass.*

It is not clear what Antonio Vivaldi may have suffered from,
and though his active service as a priest lasted only a year or
so, he was known throughout his life as "il Prete Rosso" (the
Red Priest, referring to his red hair).

While he maintained his station as chief administrator of the
seminary, Vivaldi enjoyed prolonged leaves, traveling to many
European cities as a guest conductor of orchestra and opera
performances. He was also able to fulfill other commissions
such as writing the music for the wedding of Louis XV, who
married in 1724 at the age of 14.

For most of his life, Antonio Vivaldi was considered quite
famous. His music had a significant influence on his contemporaries. But his move to Vienna, Austria in 1740 proved to
be disastrous. His genius was unrecognized there, his reputation diminished, and he died a year later in destitute
circumstances. Vivaldi's music was nearly forgotten for a
century after his death, but aroused interest with the discovery of its influence on other composers such as Johann
Sebastian Bach, who took a number of Vivaldi's violin concertos and rewrote them for the harpsichord.

Though Vivaldi wrote prolifically (nearly 50 operas, another
50 major vocal works, and 450 or so concertos, 300 of which
were for violin solo), his works are considered to be of uni-
formly high quality.

Representative Composition

FOUR SEASONS, Spring, 1st Mvt.

Type of Composition: **Concerto Grosso**

Structure: **Ritornello Form**

Inspired by a poem:
Spring has returned
And is greeted by the birds in happy song,
And fountains moved by little zephyrs
Murmur sweetly in constant flow.
When skies are mantled in black,
Lightening flashes and thunder roars.
When these have finished, little birds return
To carol their enchanting song.

TIME	TEXT	COMMENTARY
0:00	*Spring has returned*	Ritornello theme begins.
0:32	*And is greeted by the birds in happy song,*	Imitation of bird calls by three solo violins.
1:09		Ritornello returns.
1:17	*And fountains moved by little zephyrs murmur sweetly in constant flow.*	Running notes by violins, then lyrical violins over running notes by cellos.
1:41		Ritornello returns.
1:50	*When skies are mantled in black, lightening flashes and thunder roars.*	Emphasis on low pitches. Tremolo technique. Fast, upward moving scales by violins.
2:18		Ritornello returns.
2:27	*When these have finished, little birds return to carol their enchanting song.*	Imitation of bird calls by solo violins.
2:45		Ritornello returns.
2:57		Bird calls continue.
3:10		Ritornello returns.

Chapter 2

THE ELEMENTS OF MUSIC

SOUND

Sound Production and Hearing

Imagine yourself having dinner in a nice restaurant. The serene atmosphere is broken when the waiter tries to exit the kitchen just as the bus boy tries to enter. Dishes fly and there is a loud crash. What caused the noise?

Three things are needed in order for there to be sound. First, something must be set into motion — the dishes in the above scenario. Second, this movement then disturbs the surroundings and sets the air molecules into motion. And third, these molecules transfer the vibrations to the ear drum where they proceed to the inner ear and are interpreted by the brain.

On a more technical level, when something is displaced from its resting position — a dish, for example — it will push the surrounding molecules closer together, causing an increase in air pressure at that point. As those molecules are forced away, they leave a decrease in air pressure. As molecules rush in to fill this vacuum, another increase in pressure occurs and the process starts again. The result is a series of waves similar to the waves of water created when a stone is tossed into a pond. As these waves hit against the ear drum, the ear drum vibrates at the same rate of speed. In the inner ear these vibrations are detected by thousands of tiny hairlike tentacles, each of which is connected to a nerve ending which sends a message to the brain. This process sounds simple, but in reality scientists do not fully understand how we hear.

Musical Tones vs. Noise

Picture again the pond mentioned above. If a single stone is tossed into calm water, the resulting series of waves will be regular and evenly spread. If, however, a handful of gravel were thrown into the pond, the action would produce erratic and irregular water movement. The same two consequences can occur when air is disturbed. If the air molecules are displaced by something moving in a smooth consistent pattern — a string vibrating back and forth, for example, or the even undulation of a clarinet reed — the result is detected as a **musical tone**. If irregular vibrations are produced — dishes breaking, traffic in the city — **noise** is heard.

musical tone
noise

Most music that is heard on a daily basis is constructed through the combining of musical tones into compositions in which the various vibrations work together in a smooth nonabrasive fashion. However, noise, extreme clashes of vibrations, can be an effective tool of a composer wishing to create a specific emotional response. Also, commonly used instruments such as cymbals and snare drums produce sounds that are not musical tones by definition, but which richly add to the expression of musical compositions.

ELEMENTS OF A MUSICAL TONE

Every musical tone consists of four elements. The elements are **pitch, duration, dynamic level**, and **timbre**.

pitch

Pitch. Pitch is the relative *highness* or *lowness* of sound. Highness and lowness really has nothing to do with *distance above the ground*, even though the terms did originate as the Greeks were observing how some of the strings of the **lyre**

lyre

were closer to the ground than others. Musical instruments such as the flute and glockenspiel produce high pitches while the tuba and contra bassoon produce low pitches. An instrument such as the piano produces a wide spectrum of pitches from high to low. A child's voice is in the high pitch range while a man's is in the low pitch range.

frequency
vps, hz

cps

Any given pitch is measured by the rate of speed of its vibrations. This is called the **frequency** of the pitch. Frequency is generally noted using the abbreviations **vps** or **hz**. Both vps and hz represent *vibrations per second*, with vps being the direct abbreviation while hz stands for hertz, named after Heinrich Hertz, an acoustical scientist of the 19th century. Occasionally the abbreviation **cps**, representing *cycles per second*, is used synonymously with vps and hz.

It is interesting to consider the wide pitch range of human hearing. We can hear sound when the frequency is as low as 16 vps and our abilities reach as high as 20,000 vps. If we were limited to hearing only one pitch, for example, we would neither be able to understand speech as we know it, nor, of course, would we have the joy of listening to music.

duration

Duration. The second element of a musical tone is the tone's **duration**, the length of time the tone exists. Melodies consist of combinations of long tones and short tones (sometimes very long tones and sometimes very short tones). Rhythmic patterns are created by various combinations of different durations. Simultaneous combinations of varying durations often provide tools for expressive musical contrasts between melody and accompaniment.

dynamic level
dynamics

Dynamic Level. The music term **dynamic level** or often simply **dynamics** refers to loudness and softness. This element of a musical tone is created by the amount of air being disturbed when something is vibrating and by the intensity of the disturbance. Using the analogy of the pond once again, a small pebble would produce small waves while a large stone would produce bigger waves. The waves would not radiate at a faster or slower rate of speed; they would simply be of different sizes. The same is true as air molecules vibrate. A string vibrating will not push many air molecules to the ear drum, but if the string is attached to the soundboard of a piano or the soundboard of a guitar (the face of the guitar), a large amount of air is set in to motion, creating a louder sound.

decibels (db)

Dynamics are measured scientifically by what are called **decibels** (abbreviated **db**). The starting point of zero db is the point where a sound is barely loud enough to be heard. The loudest sound that a human can tolerate without physical pain is 120 db. The scale used in this system is logarithmic with each increase of 10 being ten times louder than the previous level. Thus, 50 db is ten times louder than 40 db. Most music instruments play between 40 and 80 db.

timbre

Timbre. The final element of a musical tone is **timbre** (pronounced *tamber*). This term refers to what is called tone color or tone quality. It is used in two ways. First, we might describe the timbre simply by identifying the instrument producing the tone. For example, the tone might have the timbre of a clarinet, of a violin, or of a human voice. Second, and much less specific, when we describe a sound as rich, bright, fuzzy, tinny, bassy, etc., we are describing timbre. The timbre of a voice is sometimes described as husky, nasally, full and round, raspy, clear as a bell, etc.

What causes the particular timbre of a musical tone? If the other factors are equal — same pitch, same duration, same dynamic level — why does a saxophone sound like a saxophone and not like a violin? Is it that one is made of metal and the other wood? No. (What difference would the material make since the sound is strictly vibrating air?) The answer

overtones

lies in the phenomenon of **overtones**. Any musical tone consists of what is called the *fundamental* tone *and* many, many sub vibrations. These sub vibrations are much quieter than the fundamental, but are clearly audible to the human ear. Let's look at a vibrating string (but the same thing is happening when air in a tube is activated or when one of the wooden bars of a xylophone is struck):

The string moves back and forth along its entire length, producing the *fundamental* (and the loudest) tone.

At the same time, the string vibrates exactly in half, producing a second audible pitch.

The string also divides itself into three parts, producing yet a third musical tone.

This process continues as the string vibrates in smaller and smaller parts — fourths, fifths, sixths, sevenths, etc. — infinitely.

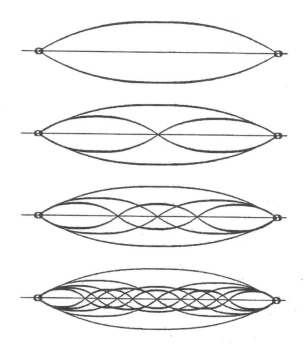

All musical instruments produce the same overtones, but the difference in instrumental timbre is created because the loudness and softness of the overtones occur in different proportions. For example, If the proportional ratio of the dynamic levels of the overtones of a banjo could be duplicated through any means, the resulting sound would be identical to (have the timbre of) a banjo — which is exactly what is done at times in the construction of electronic organs and synthesizers.

ELEMENTS OF MUSIC

Music is produced when many individual musical tones are combined in various ways. New elements are formed that are identified as the *elements of music:* Rhythm, Melody, Harmony, Texture, Form, and Style. These are briefly described below, but will be given detailed attention in future chapters.

Rhythm	The movement in music. The driving force in music. A term referring to all time aspects of music.
Melody	A succession of different pitches of varying durations perceived as an entity.
Harmony	The simultaneous sounding of two or more pitches.
Texture	The interweaving of melody, melody with harmony, and melody with melody.
Form	The elements of cohesion and structure in music.
Style	The identifiable characteristics of how an individual or many individuals employ the other elements of music.

Listening Composition

FUGUE IN G MINOR
Baroque Style Period

JOHANN SEBASTIAN BACH
1685-1750

Johann Sebastian Bach was born in Eisenach in central Germany. Although his ancestors had already produced several generations of musicians and composers, Bach was essentially self-taught. When he was very young, his father and a cousin taught him to play stringed instruments and the keyboard. But before he reached 10 years of age, Bach was orphaned. He went to live with his brother, Johann Cristoph, who was an organist at Ohrdruf. There, he learned the fundamentals of the keyboard from his brother, sang soprano in the church choir, and studied composition on his own.

In 1703, Bach accepted a position as violinist in the orchestra of the ducal court in Weimar, and six months later was appointed organist at the Neukirche in Arnstadt. It was here that he composed his earliest surviving organ works and choir cantatas.

Johann Sebastian Bach married his first cousin, Maria Barbara Bach, in 1707. That same year he was appointed organist at Saint Blasius Church in Muhlhausen. However, almost immediately, the congregation objected to his innovative music. Bach was also earning a reputation as an improviser of fugues during this time. His stint at Muhlhausen proved frustrating, and by the end of 1707, Bach moved back to Weimar to serve as the court organist. There, not being eventually granted the position of music director — a position he earnestly wanted - he began looking or a job elsewhere.

In 1717, he found a position as court conductor at Cöthen, but his request for release from his duties at Weimar was so antagonistic, he was imprisoned. The Weimar Court Secretary's report states, "On 6 November 1717 the quondam Concertmeister and organist Bach was confined to the

County Judge's place of detention for too stubbornly forcing the issue of his dismissal, and finally on December 2 was freed from arrest with notice of his unfavorable discharge." During his stay at Cöthen, Bach's wife died, leaving him with four small children. In 1721 he married Anna Magdalena Wilcken. This marriage produced 13 children, only six of whom survived. Bach remained at Cöthen until 1723.

His next position was as director of music of Saint Thomas Church in Leipzig. He was responsible for the music at the four main municipal churches. This prestigious post made him, in essence, the director of music for the entire city. Bach remained in Leipzig for 27 years, until his death. He usually composed an extended work for chorus, soloists and orchestra for each Sunday and church holiday, and he taught music to the students at Saint Thomas School.

Bach was a deeply religious man. At the beginning of his sacred compositions, he wrote the letters "J.J.," which stood for "Jesus Juva" (Jesus help); at the end of the pieces, he wrote "S.D.G.," for "Soli Deo Gloria" (to God alone the glory).

Although Bach was considered the most eminent harpsichordist, organist and improviser of his day, he was little known outside Germany, and was by no means considered the greatest composer of his day. His music was largely forgotten for many years after his death. There are some works which are thought to have been composed for Bach's own use, or for that of his friends, either because they are difficult to perform or because they are considered "clearly theoretical exercises." These works were not performed during Bach's lifetime, but today they stand as some of the most glorious works of the Baroque style period.

In the last years of his life, even though his eyesight deteriorated, Bach continued to compose, conduct and teach. By the time of his death in 1750, he was completely blind. After his death the Bach family musical dynasty continued, as several of his sons became well-known composers in their own right.

Representative Composition

FUGUE IN G MINOR

Type of Composition: **Fugue**

Structure: Alternation of fugue **subject** and **episodes**. The word "fugue" is derived from the Italian "fuga" which means "fleeing." Thus, we have the picture of something being chased by something else. This is the case in all fugues. The opening melody, called the *subject*, is presented as a single "voice." Then, the second voice enters, and, because it must follow the same "path" as the first voice (remember, it's chasing the first voice), sounds the subject. Meanwhile, the first voice continues with new musical material. This "same path" idea is a simplified way of introducing the word "imitation," i.e., the second voice *imitates* the first voice. This fugue is a "four-voice fugue." Thus, there are four entrances of the subject at the beginning. The parts then move along independently (but sometimes using bits and pieces of the subject through what is called an *episode*. Eventually, one of the voices restates the subject, followed by another episode, etc.

TIME	EVENT
0:00	Voice 1 states subject in the soprano range.
0:17	Voice 2 enters with subject melody (alto range).
0:40	Voice 3 enters with subject melody (tenor range).
0:56	Voice 4 enters with subject melody (bass range).
1:10	Episode.
1:22	Subject enters. *This statement of the subject is a little unusual because the tenor voice begins the statement, but the soprano voice takes over and completes it.
1:42	Episode.
1:50	Subject enters in alto voice.
2:13	Subject stated in bass voice.
2:30	Episode.
2:45	Subject enters in soprano voice.
3:00	Episode.
3:29	Subject enters in bass voice, then fugue is drawn to a close.

Chapter 3

MUSIC MEDIA:
VOICES & INSTRUMENTS

The transformation of a musical composition from a composer's head into physical sound requires many considerations: What is the message of the music? What emotion is to be evoked? Is the composition strictly instrumental, or are words involved? What pitch range is required? What degree of technical dexterity (speed, for example) is needed? Etc., etc. These are all questions which are answered in part by the composer's choice of sound media. The same melody, using the same pitches and rhythm, will have a wide range of emotional differences if played on oboe, trumpet, or violin.

VOICE

Ranges

The study of sound media begins with an investigation of the voice. The voice is the most natural means to communicate emotion through sound. Notice the change and control of pitch and rhythm when a person calls to another person, hits his or her thumb with a hammer, expresses sympathy, or simply asks a question. In all these instances, the person is singing!

Voices are identified by both pitch range and expressive timbre. There are three classifications for women and three

soprano
mezzo
alto /contralto
tenor
baritone
bass

for men. The highest pitch range for women is given the name **soprano**, followed by **mezzo** (pronounced *metso*) **soprano**, then the lowest, **alto** (sometimes called **contralto**). Similarly, men's voices, from highest pitches to lower are **tenor**, **baritone**, and **bass**.

The names of the voice ranges were established in the Christian church of the Middle Ages during the time when musical compositions for the worship service were expanding from single unaccompanied melodies to elaborate choir arrangements with two, three, four and more independent parts. The part that *held on to* the officially sanctioned church song was called the tenor, literally the *holder* or *holding part*. The part written higher than the main melody was called the *high part*, the alto. The word soprano means *over* or *above*, thus was placed over the alto part. (Also notice that the words are alto and soprano, not alta and soprana. This is because, at that time, only men were singing the parts.) The term mezzo soprano, with the literal meaning of mezzo being *middle* or *medium*, didn't come into existence until a later time period. Below the tenor part was the baritone part, which means the *heavy* part. Finally, because the lowest notes of a music composition have long been considered the *foundation* or *base* of the composition, comes the bass part. (The English spelling of the term *bass*, which does mean *base*, is derived from the Italian *basso*.)

Expressive Timbre

dramatic

lyric
coloratura

When describing timbres of women's voices, terms such as dramatic, lyric, and coloratura are used. A **dramatic** soprano or alto will have a powerful voice and will sing music which utilizes the lower pitch spectrum of her range. A **lyric** voice will have a lighter quality. The term **coloratura** refers to a soprano with an extremely high range and the ability to exhibit such virtuoso techniques as rapid scale passages, trills, and wide leaps.

heroic
basso profundo
basso cantante

Descriptive qualities for men's voices include, for the tenor, the terms lyric (as above) and **heroic**. A **basso profundo** demonstrates a very low powerful voice while a **basso cantante** is lighter and smoother.

boy soprano
cambiato

From an historical perspective other descriptive vocal terms are used. These include boy soprano, cambiato, castrato, countertenor, and sopranist. A **boy soprano** is, of course, a young male singing in a high pitch range. A **cambiato** is an adolescent male singer at the age when the voice is changing.

castrato

A **castrato** was a man who, during youth, had had his testicles removed in order to prevent the voice from changing. Castrati (plural of castrato) were highly praised and well-paid singers (if they sang well). Audiences enjoyed the remarkable sound produced by the large lungs of a man, but the high pitch of the voice. Castrati were most popular in the 1600's and 1700's, but the practice of performing the operation didn't cease until the twentieth century. A **countertenor** is a man who has practiced making his high *falsetto* voice (in the women's range) strong and controlled. A countertenor who specializes in singing the high parts of Middle Ages and Renaissance music is called a **sopranist**.

countertenor

sopranist

INSTRUMENTS

Typically, musical instruments are classified by the way they produce sound. For example, the word *chord* originally meant *string* (like *cord*). Therefore, instruments whose sounds are produced by vibrating strings are called **chordophones**. The other classifications are: **aerophones** (The sound is produced when *air* in an enclosed chamber is set into motion), **membranophones** (A tightly stretched *membrane* — for example, a drum head — is caused to vibrate),

chordophones
aerophones

membranophones

idiophones

electrophones

percussion instruments

idiophones (*Idio* means *self*), instruments in which the instrument itself — a cymbal, for example — is vibrating, and **electrophones**, whose sound is created through electronic means.

Below is a more detailed survey of the musical instruments. The classifications given above, while adequate in a general sense, are sometimes incomplete. Two examples: 1) The tambourine is a combination of membranophone and idiophone. 2) **Percussion instruments** are generally defined as *any instrument whose sound is produced by hitting, shaking, rattling, rubbing, or scraping*. Does this mean that a piano, whose strings are struck with hammers, is a percussion instrument?

Chordophones

Many instruments which have strings come to mind — guitar, banjo, electric bass, piano, violin, etc. All of these work in fundamentally the same way. Strings are set into motion to produce pitches. Each pitch is determined by a string's tension, density, and length. All other things being equal, greater tension will produce higher pitch. Greater density will produce lower pitch, as will greater length. Thus, given two strings of the same material and of the same length, being stretched to the same tension, the thicker string (the more dense) will produce a lower pitch. Or, think of a string on a guitar. As the tuning key is turned to tighten the tension on the string, the pitch goes up.

soundboard

But how much sound can a string produce? Not much. A string vibrating by itself is not very loud. Something else is needed in order for the instrument to be heard. That *something* is a **soundboard**. The soundboard, being much wider than a string, can move many more air molecules, resulting in a louder sound. On most instruments, a violin or guitar, for example, the part of the instrument called the *top* or *face* is the soundboard. With a piano the soundboard is a very large piece of thin wood inside the instrument which can clearly be seen near the strings. The soundboard of a banjo is made of skin or plastic. The strings of each instrument pass over a *bridge* that is attached to the soundboard. As the strings vibrate, the vibrations are transferred through the bridge and onto the soundboard. The soundboard vibrates *in sympathy with* (at the same rate of speed) as the strings and bridge, producing the same pitches, but at a louder dynamic level.

violin, viola, cello, double bass (contra bass, string bass, bass fiddle, bass viol)

The names of the conventional chordophones of the symphony orchestra are **violin, viola, cello,** and **double bass** (also called **contra bass, string bass, bass fiddle,** and **bass viol**). The soundboards of these instruments are nearly always made of spruce. The wood is very flexible, yet strong. Its fine, straight grain produces smooth, even vibrations. The back and sides of these instruments are made of a hard wood — usually maple — for the purpose of reflecting the sound back to the soundboard of the instrument in order to keep amplifying the sound.

The strings of chordophones are set into motion by a number of means — mallets, felt tipped hammers, picks, fingernails, bows, or even wind blowing across the strings. In an orchestra the string instruments are *bowed* string instruments. Each bow consists of a wooden shaft and horse hair. The coarse fibers of the horse hair, with the aid of sticky rosin placed on the hair, are scraped across the strings, grabbing and releasing each string in a series of very rapid and microscopic actions, literally *plucking* the string thousands of times with each pull of the bow.

mute

At times a **mute** will be added to a string instrument. A mute is a device that changes the timbre of the instrument and lowers the dynamic level. On the orchestral string instru-

31

ments, a mute is placed on the bridge in order to inhibit the movement of the bridge. Restricting movement of the bridge restricts, in turn, the vibrations transferred to the sound-board.

Bowed String Instruments

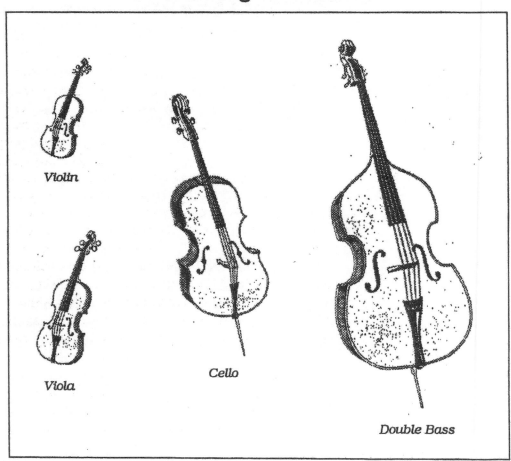

Violin

Viola

Cello

Double Bass

Aerophones

Examples of *wind instruments* are numerous — flutes, trumpets, pipe organs, saxophones, sousaphones, oboes, etc. The chamber is usually called the *air column*. It is usually cylindrical or conical in shape, but instruments such as the ocarina or even the inside design of a clarinet do not follow this rule.

Pitch is changed on the aerophones by two means: The first is to utilize different lengths of air columns. Shorter air columns produce higher pitches. Thus, some instruments are simply constructed by joining together a series of tubes of different lengths. Examples include the pipe organ, the pan pipes and the trumpet. Another way of obtaining longer or shorter lengths of air columns is to have one piece of tubing sliding over the outside of another piece. As the air vibrates in the inner tube, the outer tube can be extended to force the air to travel a longer distance before it escapes. The trombone and sackbut are examples of instruments using this method. The final way of obtaining longer or shorter lengths of air columns is to have a single tube, but to drill openings along the length of the tube. The initial vibrating column will be only as long as to the point where the air can first escape. If that opening is covered with a finger or other means, the air must travel a longer distance to the second opening. A lower pitch is the result. Flutes, oboes, and saxophones are in this category.

embouchure

The second means of changing musical tones is to force one of the overtones produced by the vibrating air to be louder than the fundamental pitch. Players do this by means of the **embouchure** (placement and pressure of the mouth and lips on the instrument). On some musical instruments a series of these overtones can be controlled well enough to provide a very wide range of pitches.

Aerophones are commonly placed into two categories, the **brass instruments** and the **woodwind instruments**.

brass instruments

Brass Instruments. On the most basic level the brass instruments are simply tubes made of brass, copper, tin, nickel, silver or some other metal. The air inside each tube is set into undulating motion by means of the buzzing of the player's lips into a cup-shaped mouthpiece. The lips must be buzzing at a frequency which corresponds to the natural frequency determined by the length of the tube or one of the overtones of that length. If the player is not trained to control the vibration of the lips in this manner, no musical tone will be produced.

The tubing may be straight or it may be curled into any shape desired. Curving the tubing will not affect the musical pitch produced because the length of the tube has not been altered.

In order to make available all pitches needed, the length of tubing is altered on the most common brass instruments by either the telescoping of one tube over another (the slide), as described above, or by a system of valves. Each valve can permit the air to either flow directly through the instrument or cause the air to flow into a piece of attached tubing. Depressing a valve will prohibit the undulating air from proceeding straight through the instrument, causing the air to be diverted onto the longer path of the additional tubing. All other things being equal, this will lower the pitch of the instrument. The most common of the brass instruments are the **trumpet, cornet, flugelhorn, French horn, trombone, baritone horn, euphonium, tuba**, and **sousaphone**.

trumpet

The **trumpet** is a member of the *bugle* family. The bugle is a curled tube with a cup-shaped mouthpiece. It has no means of lengthening or shortening the air column, thus can only produce the pitches of the natural overtone series. The trumpet consists of cylindrical tubing with the capability of three links being added by means of three valves. Because the simple addition of tubing creates problems related to the mathematical ratios of tuning one pitch with another, trumpets of professional quality also have spring-activated slides on the added tubing for more accurate pitch control. This still isn't accurate enough for the professional orchestra player who will carry several trumpets tuned in different keys to a concert in order to be as perfectly in tune as possible. The **cornet** and **flugelhorn** are constructed in the same fashion as the trumpet. The difference is that the tubing of these instruments is conical instead of cylindrical. The result is a more mellow, less piercing timbre. The diameter of the tubing of the flugelhorn is greater than that of the cornet, adding additional *fullness* (mellowness) to the tone color.

cornet
flugelhorn

While the trumpet is usually considered the soprano voice of the brass instruments, the **French horn** is the alto. Historically, before valves were placed on brass instruments in the nineteenth century, French horn players frequently utilized the high overtones of the tube. These overtones are close enough together to provide the performer with the ability to play complete melodies with only changes of embouchure. To help accomplish this, the tubing of the French horn was made narrow. The result is that, while it has the ability to play in a low pitch range, it usually sounds relatively high. Valves placed on instruments can either be *rotary* valves or *piston* valves. In Europe, rotary valves are generally preferred, but in the United States piston valves are used almost exclusively for the brass instruments, except for the French horn. It is nearly always constructed with rotary valves.

French horn

The **trombone** is the tenor voice. The cylindrical air column is made longer or shorter as the player pushes and pulls the slide, but sometimes extra tubing, controlled by a rotary valve, is added to the instrument. An instrument with the same length (and, thus, the same pitch range) as the trom-

trombone

Brass Instruments

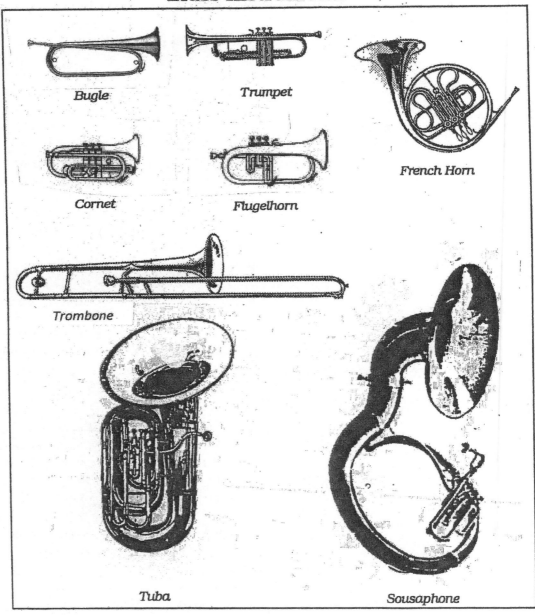

Bugle

Trumpet

French Horn

Cornet

Flugelhorn

Trombone

Tuba

Sousaphone

baritone horn

euphonium

tuba

sousaphone

helicon

woodwind instruments

aperture

bone, but utilizing a valve system like that of the trumpet, is the **baritone horn**. The baritone is seldom heard in a symphony orchestra, but is a regular member of concert and marching bands. A baritone horn with conical tubing instead of cylindrical tubing is called a **euphonium** and produces a more mellow timbre.

The lowest pitched brass instrument is the **tuba**. This bass instrument is constructed with valves in the same manner as the valved instruments discussed above. However, unlike those instruments, the tuba often has a fourth valve used to add additional tubing. An instrument of the same tube length as the tuba is the **sousaphone**. This instrument, named after the famous bandmaster John Philip Sousa, is coiled so that it can be easily carried in a marching band. Its unique shape was not the original idea of Sousa, however. An older instrument, the **helicon**, had a very similar shape.

As with the chordophones, a mute may be added to a brass instrument and serve the same two functions: To change the timbre of the instrument and to lower the dynamic level. The amount of change in each of these areas depends on the shape and construction of the mute.

Woodwind Instruments. The aerophones in the woodwind category are instruments that were either originally made of wood or that use a reed to produce the sound. They are often further identified as instruments with an **aperture**, a **single reed**, or a **double reed**.

Aperture. An aperture is a hole in an air column over which air is passed in order to disturb the air inside the column. A good example of this process is blowing across the top of a Coke bottle. As the blown air hits the edge of the opening, the air is set into motion, alternately passing outside then inside the bottle. This undulation pulsates in sympathy with the natural vibrating frequency contained in the size of the bottle (air column) producing sound waves. The sound is easy to produce, but exactly why the undulation starts in the first place is not understood by scientists. Orchestral instruments whose sound is generated by means of an aperture are the flute and piccolo. Sound is produced in this way in the air columns of a pipe organ as well.

flute

The **flute** of modern times in our society was previously called the *transverse flute* because it is held parallel to the ground as compared to *end blown* and *flageolet* (special mouthpieces which control the flow of air) instruments which are held perpendicular to the ground. Originally made of wood, the present-day flute is made of metal. Professional instruments are usually silver, but gold and platinum are sometimes used.

piccolo

The word **piccolo** is the Italian term for *little*. The musical instrument by the same name is simply a little flute. The flute itself is a soprano instrument, making the piccolo what is sometimes called a sopranino. Other members of the flute

alto flute
bass flute

family are the **alto flute** and the **bass flute**.

single reed

Single Reed. A reed is a thin rectangular-shaped piece of bamboo (cane). The reed is placed over the opening of a mouthpiece which is attached to an air column. As air is blown over the reed it begins to vibrate. It closes the opening of the mouthpiece, then opens it, closes it again, etc. in rapid succession. This action begins an undulating movement of the air inside the air column, producing sound waves. Instruments using a single reed include the clarinet and the saxophone.

clarinet

The **clarinet**, developed in the 1690's from an instrument called the *chalumeau*, did not become a regular member of the symphony orchestra until almost a century later when Wolfgang Amadeus Mozart began utilizing it in symphonic and chamber music. Traditionally, it has been made of very dense ebony or grenadilla wood, but in modern times inexpensive clarinets are made of plastic, ebonite, or some other synthetic material. The clarinet is interesting from an acoustical viewpoint. Because of the combination of single reed and cylindrical air chamber, every other overtone is prohibited from escaping. Thus, for example, while a person who knows how to play the flute also knows the basic fingerings of the saxophone and oboe, that person will find that clarinet fingering doesn't follow the same pattern.

sopranino, soprano, alto, bass, and contrabass clarinet

The instrument referred to simply as the clarinet is really a soprano clarinet. In addition to this instrument are the very small **sopranino clarinet**, the larger **alto clarinet**, the even larger **bass clarinet**, and the very large **contrabass clarinet**.

saxophone

The **saxophone**, widely used in jazz and popular music, is not a traditional member of a symphony orchestra. It was originally invented for a very special purpose: Military bands were very popular in Europe in the middle 1800's. Being used outdoors, the wood of the clarinet was subject to the extremes of the weather — rain, sun, low temperatures, etc. Also, the clarinet was not loud enough to hold a place along side the brass instruments. So, instrument maker Adolf Sax set out to invent an instrument that had the timbre of a reed instrument, but that was louder and could endure outdoor conditions. The result, the saxophone, was patented in 1845. It uses a single reed like the clarinet, is made of metal like the brass instruments, and is formed in the shape of a megaphone in order for the sound to be very loud.

sopranino, soprano, alto, tenor, baritone, bass, and contrabass saxophone

The saxophone family of instruments includes the names **sopranino**, **soprano**, **alto**, **tenor**, **baritone**, **bass**, and **contrabass**. The most commonly heard saxophones are the alto and tenor, but currently the soprano saxophone is very popular. The contrabass saxophone is so large that it is seldom picked up by the player. The instrument is usually set on a little cart with wheels to be rolled around as the performer desires.

double reed

Double Reed. Placing two single reeds together forms a double reed. The natural curve of the two pieces of cane, when placed in opposing positions, form an opening between the two through which air is blown. The air makes the reeds vibrate against each other, causing the opening to close, open, close, open, etc. in undulating fashion. When the reeds are attached to an air column, the air will begin to undulate with the reeds. The main instruments of the double reed group are the oboe, English horn, bassoon and contra bassoon.

oboe

The **oboe** is heard in nearly all symphonic literature. Descended from an instrument called the *shawm*, the timbre of the oboe is rich and penetrating. A single oboe can be heard above the simultaneous playing of many string instruments. The richness of the timbre is created by the prominence of many of the strong overtones. This timbre makes it easy for the player to focus on the fundamental pitch and maintain it with security. For this reason, the entire orchestra tunes to the oboe. The literal meaning of the word oboe is *high wood*. It is a soprano instrument. The alto counterpart is the

English horn

English horn. The name is a misnomer. The instrument is French, but the part of the instrument that holds the reed is *angled*. The name *angled horn* became mistakenly called the *Anglo* (English) horn.

bassoon

The tenor of the double reeds is the **bassoon**. It has a very wide range of pitches, but because of the prominence of the overtones, building a bassoon is not as simple as just building a big oboe. The instrument would be terribly out of tune. Thus, to compensate for the irregularities of the pitches, the bassoon has many keys in order to adjust the individual pitches. (The player's left thumb alone is responsible for

Woodwind Instruments

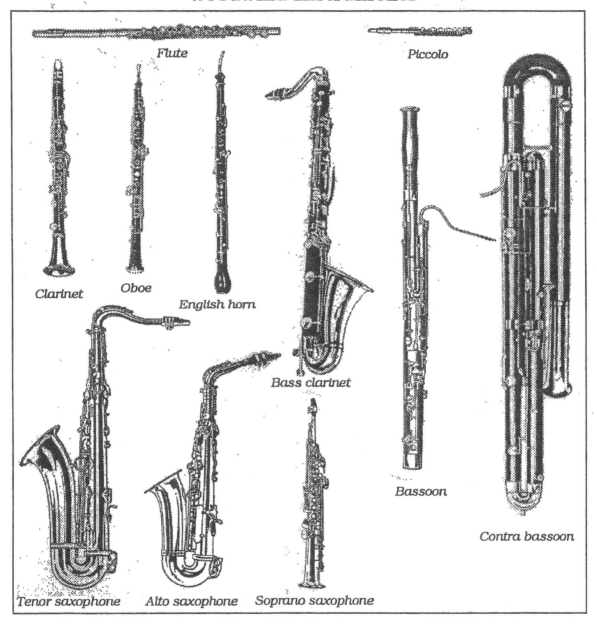

Flute

Piccolo

Clarinet

Oboe

English horn

Bass clarinet

Bassoon

Contra bassoon

Tenor saxophone

Alto saxophone

Soprano saxophone

contra bassoon

seven different keys.) Lower in range than the bassoon is the **contra bassoon.** In fact, the contra bassoon can produce the lowest pitch of any instrument in the orchestra.

Membranophones

Membranophones are drums. Even though in other cultures there exist such instruments as log drums and string drums, in Western culture a drum has a skin or synthetic membrane called the *drum head*. This is the part of the instrument that

snare drum

is struck to produce the sound. The **snare drum** has two heads. As one head is struck, the other head also vibrates. Thin wires called snares, placed against this second head, rattle when this head moves. This gives the snare drum its characteristic timbre. A snare drum without the snares is

tom tom
bass drum

called a **tom tom** drum (though present-day tom toms often only have one head). The **bass drum** is a large tom tom drum. Other membranophones include the bongo and conga drums.

One membranophone is distinctive because, unlike the drums mentioned above, it produces tones of definite pitch. Historically, this drum was never used singly, thus the plural

timpani

Italian name **timpani** identified the instruments. Although it is a misnomer, the name now often refers to just one drum.

kettledrums

Another name for timpani is **kettledrum.**

Idiophones

The association of the term *idiophone* with such instruments

cymbals, triangle,
gong, tam tam,
castanets, claves,
maracas, guiro,
church bell

as **cymbals, triangle, gong, tam tam, castanets, claves, maracas, guiro,** and **church bells** is clearly understood. The bodies of the instruments themselves vibrate to produce the sound. It is not as easy to see that the **xylophone, marimba, vibraphone (vibraharp), glockenspiel, orchestral bells, celeste, tubular bells, accordion, harmonica,** etc. are also in this category. These instruments are made of many individual idiophones placed on some kind of frame or support.

xylophone, marimba, vibraphone (vibraharp), glockenspiel, orchestral bells, celeste, tubular bells (chimes), accordion, harmonica

chimes

Examine the xylophone and marimba: Considering that a rectangularly-shaped piece of wood will vibrate just like a string vibrates, such pieces can be cut to various lengths to correspond to musical pitches. These strips are then attached to a frame and are struck with a mallet. The same is even true if metal is the material being used. With instruments such as the glockenspiel, orchestral bells, and vibraphone, relatively thick pieces of metal of various sizes are placed together. The celeste also uses vibrating metal as the sound source, but it uses long thin strips of the material. A keyboard with hammers which looks identical to a piano keyboard is the means by which the player sets the metal strips into motion. The tubular bells (also known as the **chimes**) is also an instrument in which metal is vibrating. In this case, however, the lengths corresponding to the musical tones are in the form of tubes. The player uses a wooden hammer to strike the tubes. The use of tubes brings about another interesting consideration: Tubes are air columns (as described with the aerophones above). When a tube of the orchestral bells is struck, the pitch produced is determined by the length and density of the metal. However, the size of the air column has been designed to correspond with the same pitch. Thus, the moving metal will also cause the air inside the tube to vibrate at the same frequency, reinforcing and resonating the sound. The air columns, visible underneath the wooden bars of the xylophone and marimba, serve the same purpose.

On first thought the accordion and harmonica would seem to be aerophones, but they are, in fact, idiophones. Although metal reeds in the instruments are activated by air, the reeds themselves produce the sound, not air vibrating in a chamber. The reeds are of different size, corresponding to the various musical tones, in the same way as the xylophone, orchestral bells, etc. mentioned above.

Percussion Instruments

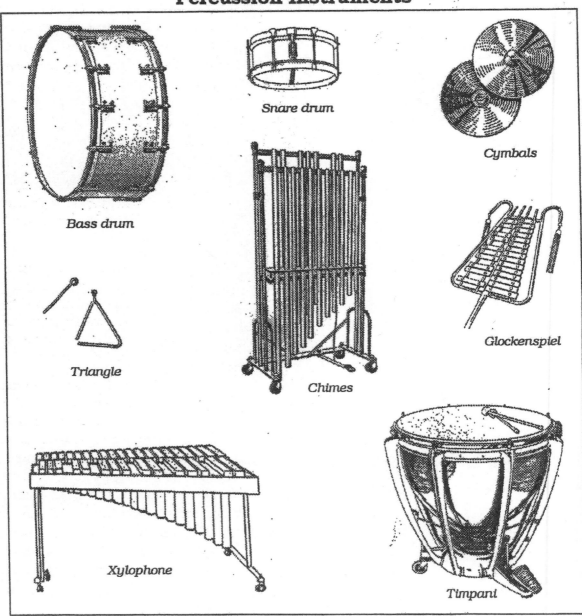

Bass drum

Snare drum

Cymbals

Triangle

Chimes

Glockenspiel

Xylophone

Timpani

PERFORMING GROUPS

While any combination of voices and/or instruments is possible, some have become standardized. Just mentioning the name of the combination identifies the instrumentation of the combination. Below are some of the most common performing groups.

string quartet
piano trio
piano quintet
brass quartet

woodwind quintet

A **string quartet** consists of two violins, a viola, and a cello. A **piano trio** is not three pianos, but consists of piano, violin, and cello. Similarly, a **piano quintet** is a piano with a string quartet. A **brass quartet** is composed of trumpet, French horn, trombone, and tuba — all brass instruments — but a **woodwind quintet** has flute, oboe, clarinet, French horn, and bassoon.

chorale
chorus
choir
a cappella
a cappella choir

Vocal ensembles of a mix of both men and women singers might have the name **chorale**, **chorus**, or **choir**. A vocal group singing without instrumental accompaniment is said to be singing **a cappella**. This term is often attached to the word choir, i. e., an **a cappella choir**, but the names *a cappella chorale* and *a cappella chorus are* seldom used.

concert band
wind ensemble
symphony orchestra

In large performing ensembles such as the **concert band** (also called a **wind ensemble**) and **symphony orchestra**, the number of each type of instrument and the instrument's placement on stage is based on the objective of being able to hear the instruments in balanced proportions. For example, a violin produces a much softer sound than a trumpet. Therefore, in a symphony orchestra, there will be many more violins than trumpets, and the violinists sit closer to the front of the stage. The high pitch of a triangle is distinctly heard, even when the rest of the orchestra is playing. Thus, a lone triangle player can be placed at the back of the stage.

Below are typical seating arrangements for a symphony orchestra and a concert band. Variations will occur, depend-

45

ing on the wishes of the conductor when considering musical style and interpretation.

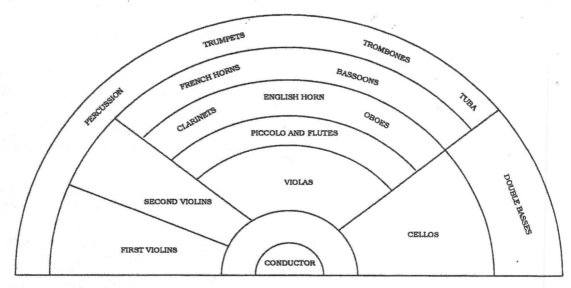

Symphony Orchestra

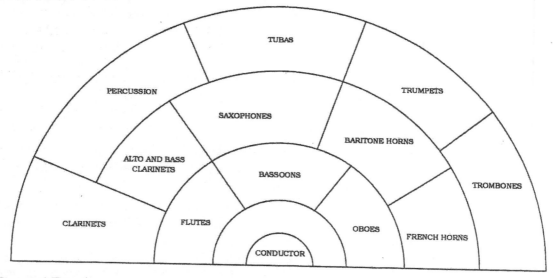

Concert Band

Listening Composition

MESSIAH: *Hallelujah*
Baroque Style Period

GEORGE FRIDERIC HANDEL
1685-1759

George Frideric Handel was born in Halle, Germany. He began a serious study of music at age nine and demonstrated outstanding talent at the keyboard. At age eleven, he began composing and giving organ lessons. A year later, he became the assistant organist at the cathedral at the University of Halle, and at age seventeen he was appointed principal organist.

Handel moved to Hamburg in 1703 to study opera, and to play harpsichord and violin in the opera orchestra. Considered a strong-willed individual, Handel was once challenged to a duel over who should play harpsichord at an opera. Luckily, his opponent's sword was broken by a button on Handel's coat.

In 1706, Handel traveled to Italy, and remained there for four years. During this time, he composed his first two oratorios and many widely-acclaimed operas. These important pieces bring to light Handel's increasing mastery of Italian style.

Handel returned to Germany in 1710 and became musical director to the elector of Hanover. He was well paid for this position. After only a month, he asked for a leave of absence to go to London, where his opera Rinaldo was being performed with immense success. Returning briefly to Hanover, he again requested a leave. This leave was granted for a "reasonable time" — which turned out to be for the rest of Handel's life. Deciding to remain in this far away country without having requested a formal dismissal, imagine Handel's surprise when his former employer suddenly became King George I of England. Managing to make amends with the king, Handel was granted many special favors. London became his permanent home, and Handel became an English citizen in 1727.

Though he continued to compose in the Italian style, Handel absorbed certain characteristics of English music. He became musical director of the Royal Academy of Music in 1719 and continued in that position until this commercial opera company folded in 1728. He then formed his own company in order to produce his works. The so-called Second Academy operated from 1728 to 1734, eventually going bankrupt. This apparent disaster was actually a boon to Handel and, ultimately, the world of music. After initially suffering a breakdown, Handel continued producing his operas, but decided to also present his oratorios, for which he eventually became far better known.

George Frideric Handel's famous oratorio *Messiah* lasts approximately 2 1/2 hours. It was composed in roughly three weeks. The first performance was in Dublin as a benefit for people in debtor's prison. It ran for six consecutive nights in a hall which normally seated 600 people. But the rehearsals drew so much attention that, in an effort to increase the room capacity, women were asked not to wear hoop skirts and men were requested to leave their swords at home.

After the first performance of *Messiah* in London, Handel remarked to Lord Kinnoull, "I should be sorry, my lord, if I have only succeeded in entertaining them; I wished to make them better." If you ever see a performance of this piece, you may wonder why people stand during the "Hallelujah" chorus. When King George II heard it, he was so moved that he rose from his seat. When a king rises, everyone must follow suit. Thereafter, it become a tradition associated with that portion of the oratorio.

When George Frideric Handel died in 1759, over 3,000 mourners came to his funeral at Westminster Abbey.

Representative Composition

MESSIAH: Hallelujah

Type of Composition: **Oratorio excerpt for chorus and orchestra**

Structure: The words being sung dictate the musical material. New melodic statements are presented for each of the four "subtopics" of the text. However, the music is not fragmented. It is strongly unified by the recurrence of the introductory "Hallelujah" melody. Throughout this composition, word painting (the use of melodic and rhythmic elements to describe the feeling and meaning of the words) is prominent.

TIME	TEXT	COMMENTARY
0:00		Orchestral introduction.
0:06	*Hallelujah! Hallelujah! Hallelujah! Hallelujah! Hallelujah!*	Chorus enters using the same melody as was heard in the introduction. The use of syncopation, along with the quicker rhythm on the third and fourth statement of "Hallelujah," create a feeling of spontaneity and enthusiasm, corresponding to the meaning of the words ("Praise the Lord"). Also at these two places, the orchestral accompaniment changes rhythm to "echo" the vocal rhythm, adding to the uplifting spirit.
0:14	*Hallelujah! Hallelujah! Hallelujah! Hallelujah! Hallelujah!*	Repetition of the above, but starting on a higher pitch. The higher pitch adds more excitement.
0:23	*For the Lord God omnipotent reigneth.*	All voices and instruments combine to sound a new melody without the use of harmony. Handel's choice to present the words in this way creates power (the word "omnipotent" means "all powerful") and unity (the Old Testament Shema [recited by Jews and Christians] declares "Hear, O Israel: The Lord is Our God; the Lord is <u>One</u>").

0:45		The fast rhythm of "Hallelujah" is combined with the slower, powerful rhythm of "Lord God Omnipotent" to form an intertwining of the previously heard melodies.
1:10	*The kingdom of this world is become the Kingdom of our Lord and of His Christ.*	A new melody is introduced. As the words "of this world" are presented, the melodic direction is downward (the earth is thought of as down' Heaven is up) and soft (weak). "The Kingdom of our Lord" is very loud (strong) and the melodies for the two statements of "and of His Christ". ascend.
1:28	*And He shall reign for ever and ever.*	The words are presented as the beginning of a four-part fugue, the entrances of the "subject" entering in the order bass, tenor, alto, soprano, The movement is, again, ascending.
1:48	*King of Kings, and Lord of Lords, for ever and ever. Hallelujah!*	Long tones of "King of Kings" are answered by the familiar melody and rhythm of "Hallelujah" established at the beginning. The pitch level and musical intensity continue to ascend.
2:26	*And He shall reign for ever and ever. King of Kings, and Lord of Lords, for ever and ever. Hallelujah!*	The "fugue" began previously on these words, and the power and spontaneity of the "King of Kings..." statement combine with the "Hallelujah" motive to build the dramatic finish.

Chapter 4

RHYTHM

rhythm

Rhythm is a Greek word meaning *flow*. Thus, it pertains to motion, movement, and momentum — music passing through time. In reality it is difficult to define exactly what rhythm is because it encompasses such a wide range of considerations. These include the beat, speed, meter, and the individual durations of each pitch. If these were the only factors, it would be easy to define rhythm as *a term referring to the time aspects of music*. But there is more. The energy and momentum sometimes felt in a music performance or the undefinable command of the musical flow that exceptional performers can sometimes convey to the listeners lead to another definition: **Rhythm** *is the driving force in music.*

BEAT

beat
pulse

Often, an easily discernible aspect of music is the beat. The **beat** is the steady, recurring pulsation heard in a song. Also known as the **pulse**, the beat divides time into equal segments. It is what we normally tap our feet or snap our fingers to.

strong beat
direct beat

If the beat is very precise, clear, and easily discernible, the music is said to contain a **strong beat**, sometimes called a **direct beat**. This aspect of popular music has been given so much emphasis that it is sometimes mistakenly used to define rhythm, as in the expression, *The music had a good* *rhythm to it.* What is meant in that statement is, *The music had a strong beat.*

However, at times, the beat may not be easily detected. In those instances it may be that the music is not intended to have a steady pulse at all, or that the desired expression places the pulse in a less prominent role. In this latter instance the music is said to have a **weak beat** or an **indirect beat.**

weak beat
indirect beat

CHANGES OF THE BEAT

When a steady pulse is present, be it a strong pulse or a weak pulse, it may undergo changes during the course of the musical composition. The beat may make abrupt changes, for example from fast to slow, or fast to very fast. But abrupt changes are not as common as varying degrees of gradual change. If the beat gradually becomes slower, the process is known as **ritardando.** For expressive purposes a ritardando may be used at any place in a piece of music, but most commonly it is used at the end of main divisions in the music and at the very end. The gradual speeding up of the beat is called **accelerando.** Accelerando is not used as often as ritardando, but it can be extremely effective if the desire is to add excitement to the music. If, at a specific moment in the music, the sound is prolonged or suspended to the point that the beat completely stops, this holding of the sound is known as **fermata.** A fermata is often found on the very last note of a song in order to create a feeling of dramatic finality. Ferma-tas are also used in musical introductions and climax points. Examples of the latter are the long-held pitch on *FREE* in *Land of the FREE* of our national anthem and, when "Johnny" has a birthday, the *-NY* part of *Happy birthday dear John-NY.*

ritardando

accelerando

fermata

More subtle changes of the beat are experienced when a technique of performance called rubato is used. **Rubato** is

rubato

the *very slight* speeding up *and* slowing down of the beat. Usually experienced in slow compositions, the performer takes liberties with the expected regularity of the pulse for expressive purposes. Coming from the Italian word meaning *to rob*, the idea is: If something is taken from the beat (the music slows down), the beat should be repaid what it lost (the music speeds up). Thus, the steadiness of the pulse fluctuates a little or a lot, depending on the amount of rubato being applied.

TEMPO

tempo

The common definition of **tempo** is *the relative rate of speed*. Thus, a composition might have a tempo that is fast, slow, moderately fast, very slow, etc. But in music, the concept of tempo also includes certain elements of the feeling and character of the music. This is observed in the use of the Italian *tempo* terms. The terms, with three exceptions, do not describe *rate of speed* as much as they describe the underlying expression attempting to be conveyed.

grave	solemn, serious, grave, deep, heavy
largo	broad, wide, large
lento	slow
adagio	at ease, in a graceful manner, gently
andante	walking, strolling
moderato	moderately
allegro	happy, cheerful, merry
vivace	lively, vivacious, sprightly
presto	fast

The meaning of the above terms can be amplified by placing them together (i.e., allegro–vivace); joining them with other Italian terms such as *molto* (*very*, i.e., molto lento) and *piu* (*more*, i.e., piu allegro); or adding the diminutives *-etto* or *-ino*

53

(i.e., *allegretto* and *andantino*) or the superlative *-issimo* (i.e., *prestissimo*). This process can even be carried to extremes — if you consider *prestississississimo* an extreme.

METER

While it is relatively easy to identify a strong steady beat in a song, closer attention will reveal that in most of the music we listen to, the beats are also grouped into recurring patterns. Think about marching to the Mickey Mouse Club song as written below. Place emphasis on the capitalized words.

Sing:	WHO'S the leader	OF the	club that's MADE for	you and	ME - - - - - - - -	
March:	LEFT Right	LEFT	Right LEFT	Right LEFT	Right	

meter

Notice how there is a stress on the placing of each *Left* foot and less of a stress on each *Right* foot. Thus, a pattern of STRONG – weak – STRONG – weak is created. The grouping of beats into regular recurring patterns is called **meter**.

duple meter

Furthermore, the STRONG – weak – STRONG – weak pattern of the Mickey Mouse Club song could be counted ONE – two – ONE – two. When the beats of a song are organized in groups of two's, the song is in **duple meter**.

Now examine the song MY COUNTRY 'TIS OF THEE. It wouldn't feel right to march to this song, as illustrated below:

Sing:	MY	coun – try	'TIS	of	thee	SWEET	land	of	LIB	–	er –	ty
March:	LEFT	Right LEFT	Right	LEFT	Right	LEFT	Right	LEFT	Right	LEFT	Right	

The organization of ONE – two – ONE – two does not fit MY COUNTRY 'TIS OF THEE. The beats of the song are grouped ONE – two – three – ONE – two – three. Tap your feet to confirm that the following organization works better:

Sing:	MY	coun – try	'TIS	of	thee	SWEET	land	of	LIB	–	er –	ty
March:	LEFT	Right Right	LEFT	Right	Right	LEFT	Right	Right	LEFT	Right	Right	

triple meter

When the beats of a song are organized in groups of three's, the song is in **triple meter**.

quadruple meter

Most music that is heard on a daily basis, whether classical music, jazz, folk, rock, country-western, etc., is in either duple or triple meter. In music writing, it is common to indicate a beat grouping of four's — **quadruple meter** — but four is just two times two. Any song in quadruple meter can be analyzed as *duple meter*. In fact, it is often difficult for trained musicians to hear any distinction.

**asymmetrical beat
changing meter**

Other beat groupings are occasionally heard. A grouping of five beats, seven beats, eleven beats, etc., will usually simply be identified as an **asymmetrical meter**. If the meter changes within a musical composition, the term **changing meter** is used.

SYNCOPATION

As noted above, meter sets up a natural pattern of strong and weak beats. If the natural stress is shifted from the strong beat to the weak beat, a unique effect is created that can be of importance in musical expression. Try shifting the accents of the Mickey Mouse Club song as written below. As before, place emphasis on the capitalized words.

Sing:	Who's the	LEADER	of	the	CLUB	that's	Made for	YOU	and	Me	–	EE
March:	*Left*	*RIGHT*	*Left*		*RIGHT*		*Left*	*RIGHT*		*Left*		*RIGHT*
Count:	One	TWO	One		TWO		One	TWO		One		TWO

syncopation

This placing of stress on a beat or part of a beat that is normally not emphasized is called **syncopation**.

Now, let's examine the *part of the beat* aspect of syncopation: In a song like THIS OLD MAN, the accents of the music correspond exactly to the natural stresses found in the words. (As before, marching to the music helps you *feel* the beat.)

Sing:	This	old	man,	he	played	one;	he	played	knick-knack	on	my	thumb
March:	LEFT		Right	LEFT		Right	LEFT		Right	LEFT		Right
Count:	ONE		Two	ONE		Two	ONE		Two	ONE		Two

If the composer of CAMPTOWN RACES had treated that song's words in the same way, the result would be:

Sing:	Camptown	la – dies	sing	this	song,	Doo	–	Dah,	Doo	–	Dah
March:	LEFT	Right	LEFT	Right	LEFT	Right		LEFT			Right
Count:	ONE	Two	ONE	Two	ONE	Two		ONE			Two

But, the composer chose to place the two *Dah's* quickly after beat *one* of each group, creating a little tension, due to the anticipation of beat *two*.

Sing:	Camptown	la – dies	sing	this	song,	Doo – Dah,		Doo – Dah
March:	LEFT	Right	LEFT	Right	LEFT	Right	LEFT	Right
Count:	ONE	Two	ONE	Two	ONE	Two	ONE	Two

The special attention given to the *Dah's*, when placed in between the beats, creates syncopation. As is generally the case, the emphasis at these normally-not-accented places adds momentum and rhythmic drive to the musical effect. This type of syncopation is commonly found in American jazz and spirituals. Examine the following:

THIS TRAIN

Sing:	This	train	is	bound	for glo – ry,	This train -
Count:	ONE	Two	ONE	Two	ONE	Two	ONE	Two

WHEN THE SAINTS GO MARCHING IN

Sing:	Lord, I	want	to be	in that	num–ber - - - - - - - - - - - - - - - - -
Count:	ONE	Two	ONE	Two	ONE	Two	ONE	Two

SWING LOW, SWEET CHARIOT

Sing:	Com– in'	for' to	car – ry	me home -
Count:	ONE	Two	ONE	Two	ONE	Two	ONE	Two

56

Listening Composition

SYMPHONY NO. 94, 2ⁿᵈ mvt.
Classical Style Period

FRANZ JOSEPH HAYDN
1732-1809

Born in Rohrau, Austria to amateur musicians in March, 1732, Franz Joseph Haydn is considered one of the greatest composers of the Classical period.

During the 1740's, he sang in the choir in Saint Stephen's Cathedral in Vienna. But when his voice changed during his teenage years, he was dismissed from the school. Penniless, he took odd jobs, including playing the violin in street bands and teaching music to children. He struggled to purchase his own textbooks in order to pursue the study of composition and music theory.

Haydn's self-teaching and hard work paid off. In 1758, he became the musical director for Count Ferdinand Maximilian von Morzin at his estate in Bohemia. In 1761, he entered the service of Prince Paul Anton Esterhazy, a wealthy and powerful nobleman with a passion for music. When Prince Paul Anton died in 1762, Prince Nicolaus continued to enjoy the service Haydn provided. The Esterhazy family remained Haydn's patron for the rest of his life.

One of the Esterhazy palaces, Esterhaza at Eisenstadt, was where Haydn spent much of his time. The palace contained a theater, an opera house, two concert halls, and 126 guest rooms. Haydn's duties included composing all the music requested by his patrons, coaching singers, overseeing the instruments and music library, and conducting the orchestra. There was usually daily chamber music, and two concerts and two operas performances weekly. Although this is a phenomenal amount of work, Haydn performed his duties conscientiously. He was professional, and always concerned about his musicians. Haydn was considered good-humored and unselfish.

In 1790, Prince Anton Esterhazy succeeded Prince Nicolaus. The new prince cared little for music. Though he retained Haydn as his musical director, he required little of him. This radical change provided Haydn a great opportunity to compose and travel as he wished.

Through the years, even with all of his duties at the palace, Haydn was still able to maintain contact with the musical world in nearby Vienna. His friendship with Wolfgang Amadeus Mozart was beneficial and influential for both men. Like Mozart, Haydn wrote nearly every conceivable form of music. A Catholic, he was profoundly moved by Handel's *Messiah*. He wrote masses, oratorios, and other religious compositions for church and concert performance. When he was criticized for writing religious music that was too "happy," Haydn replied that he didn't believe the Lord minded cheerful music.

Haydn is widely known for his invention and experimentation in music. He hated arbitrary "rules" of composition. He believed that the science of composition would not tolerate "technical chains." He said, "Art is free. The educated ear is the sole authority. And I think that I have as much right to lay down the law as anyone."

Representative Composition

SYMPHONY NO. 94, 2nd Mvt.

Type of Composition: **Movement from a symphony**

Structure: **Theme and Variations.** The "theme and variations" form consists of presenting song (the theme), then repeating the song over and over, but with various changes (the variations). This form is sometimes outlined A A$_1$ A$_2$ A$_3$, etc., with the theme represented by "A" and the variations represented by the subscripts. The theme itself of this movement of the Haydn symphony has a clearly-defined form. It consists of two parts, outlined "ab" (lower-case letters are used here to distinguish the internal form of the theme from the overall form of the entire movement). But, each part is repeated, resulting in "aabb" (the "surprise" chord occurs at the end of the second "a").

TIME	EVENT	SEGMENT OF aabb FORM	COMMENTARY
0:00	**Theme**	a	The melody is built on a seven-note motive (six short notes and a long one). The overall direction of the motive is upward. The melodic movement is primarily disjunct. This segment = motive + inversion of the motive + motive + phrase ending.
0:16		a	Repeat of "a," but softer and with the surprise chord at the end.
0:33		b	This new segment is a contrast to "a." The disjunct movement continues at first (though the notes are connected more smoothly), but the melodic direction is downward. Then a return to the motive (almost—it is an imitation) results in a climax created by a high note, followed by an ending in conjunct movement (the longest series of conjunct pitches thus far).
0:50		b	Repeat of "b," but with the addition of flute and oboe.
1:07	**Variation 1**	a	The theme is varied by 1) strong chords at the beginning, and 2) a newly-composed countermelody.
1:24		a	Repeat of "a."
1:41		b	New countermelody.
1:58		b	Repeat of "b."

2:14	**Variation 2**	a	Theme presented with the dressing of the "dark" sound of a minor key, but ends in a new major key.
2:30		a	Repeat of "a."
2:47		b	Many changes begin to occur here. The harmony is not consistent with the previous "b" segments, but the downward direction is. Instead of the usual "b" followed by its repetition, Haydn combines them into one unit, making it difficult to tell where the second "b" begins.
3:02		b	An important climax, identified by a ritardando, unison melody (no harmony) and an inversion of the motive, leads directly into the next variation.
3:22	**Variation 3**	a	Notes of the motive are doubled.
3:38		a	Instead of repeating "a," a new variation is stated.
3:56		b	A strong connection between this segment and the previous "a" is created by maintaining the same instrumentation.
4:13		b	Repeat of "b," but with the addition of French horns.
4:30	**Variation 4**	a	Loud, full orchestra (including timpani). The theme is carried by low-pitched instruments while fast notes are played by higher-pitched ones.
4:46		a	A new variation is begun. This contrasts the first "a" by means of soft dynamics and smooth movement.
5:03		b	A continuation of the character of the second "a."
5:21		b	A loud, full orchestra returns to the character of the first "a" of this variation.
5:36	**Ending**		The ending is introduced without a break in the music. Intensity is created by loudness and the use of only fragments of the motive.
5:45			Fermata. This climax point occurs at a loud dynamic level followed by a noticeable silence.
5:50			Fragments of motive continue until end.

Chapter 5
MELODY

Some people consider melody the most important aspect of music. Certainly it is the part of a song that we hum, whistle, and recognize easily. Some melodies are short little catchy tunes, while others are long and elaborate. As you listen to melodies, focus on the following components.

MELODIC MOVEMENT

Melodic Range

melodic range

The degree of highness and lowness of the pitches used in a melody is called the **melodic range**. When listening to music, does the melody stay within a relatively small area, or does it use extremes? Sing the songs JINGLE BELLS and THE STAR SPANGLED BANNER. The former has a rather narrow melodic range while the latter is very wide.

Conjunct and Disjunct Movement

conjunct movement
disjunct movement

As a melody moves from one pitch to another, does it move to a nearby pitch, or does it skip over some pitches in order to arrive at the second pitch? If the pitches generally move to nearby neighbors, the motion of the melody is described as **conjunct movement**. If the pitches primarily leap around as they travel, the motion is described as **disjunct movement**. The difference between conjunct and disjunct movement can be heard in the songs ARE YOU SLEEPING and SKIP TO MY LOU.

61

ARE YOU SLEEPING is primarily conjunct, except at the very end of the song — the *bell ringing* part. SKIP TO MY LOU, containing many skips, is primarily disjunct — probably to help describe the word *skip* in the song. The movement of most songs will not be totally conjunct or totally disjunct. A combination of the two adds variety to the melody. Also, since most melodies are associated with the idea of being easy to remember and easy to sing, most melodies will tend to be more conjunct than disjunct.

Melodic Contour

Often, a melody will have a distinctive shape to it. Consider the song JOY TO THE WORLD:

Joy to the world, the Lord is come,   let earth   re-ceive   her King

The melody, starting on a higher pitch, progresses downward until the word *come*. This downward movement parallels the image of the Lord coming down to earth. Then, the melody ascends, possibly with the picture of the earth reaching up to *receive her King*, or with the idea of a *King* being above his people. The shape of a melody is known as the **melodic contour.**

melodic contour

Most songs will not have a melodic contour as obvious and straight forward as JOY TO THE WORLD, but most songs will have definite patterns of shape that give the songs feelings of direction and continuity. For example, can there be any doubt that the arching shapes of the song SOMEWHERE OVER THE RAINBOW were intended to describe a rainbow? Or, that the leap upward from the word *way* to *up high* is using the melodic contour to musically state what the words are saying?

Some – where   ov – er the rain–bow way   up   high

Climax Point

climax point

Another consideration of melodic analysis is that of a point of great tension or emphasis. This point is called the **climax.** It is easy to identify the climax points of POP GOES THE WEASEL, HAPPY BIRTHDAY TO YOU and THE STAR SPANGLED BANNER. The common techniques used to bring music to a climax are the use of a high pitch, a change in the rhythmic activity (faster notes or a long sustained note) and an increase in the loudness of the music, but harmony and timbre can also be effective tools.

Notice that the climaxes of the above-mentioned songs occur near the end of the songs. This is the most typical place to put the climax, just like the main climax in a novel or movie. But with the song SOMEWHERE OVER THE RAINBOW, the strongest point is at the beginning of the song — like forming the high arch of a rainbow. This is followed by a second, smaller climax — like a smaller rainbow.

KEY CENTER

Tonality

keynote
keytone
key

Music of Western civilization, regardless of the style of music, generally gives one pitch more importance than all the other pitches. This main pitch, from where we get the word **keynote** or **keytone** and, ultimately, simply the word **key**, is felt most strongly at the end of a musical composition. Sing any song and stop one note before the end. A strong sensation of incompleteness is felt. But is this because the words to the song are incomplete? Try singing the song without words, or

tonal center
tonal music
tonality

better yet, try making up a melody. You will always feel a strong pull to one final pitch that seems to complete the melody. The pull to this keytone creates what is known as **tonal center**. Music with a tonal center is known as **tonal music**, and the overall concept is called **tonality**.

To make music compositions interesting, usually the feeling of the keytone is firmly established at the beginning, then tension and release are created as the music moves away from the keytone, then back in alternating fashion until the final resolution on the keytone at the very end.

What causes this pull to the keytone and the resolution that is felt at its arrival? To answer this question it is necessary to look at the individual pitches of our music system:

In the Middle Ages, when music in western Europe was just beginning to be written down and scrutinized, the pitches in use at the time were placed in progressive order from low to high. The following rectangles could represent the pitches placed side by side.

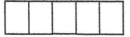

Following the tradition of the Greeks, the pitches were identified by letter names:

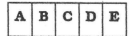

A curious phenomenon was noticed as the letter names were applied. Progressing up the alphabet, it was noticed that upon arriving at the eighth pitch, that pitch sounded almost identical to the first pitch. Therefore, this pitch was given the same letter name as the first pitch:

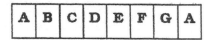

It was also noticed that, at this point, the music system started over. Therefore, the complete system of pitches of the Middle Ages was as follows:

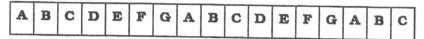

A	B	C	D	E	F	G	A	B	C	D	E	F	G	A	B	C

octave

Thus, the music alphabet consisted, and still consists, of the letters **A B C D E F G**. From any given tone, a tone with the same letter name will be found eight tones away. This distance is called an **octave**. Acoustically, the reason that the pitches at the distance of an octave sound so similar is that the vibrations of the higher pitch are exactly twice those of the lower pitch.

However, the question about the pull to a keytone still hasn't been answered. Let's continue. As the pitches of our music system were more carefully analyzed, it was discovered that, although they appear to be equidistant, they are not. The distance between the adjacent pitch **E** and **F** and the pitches **B** and **C** are closer together than other adjacent pitches. In fact, according to our present system, they are exactly half the distance, which means that if we were to add pitches in order to make all spaces equal, there is room for other pitches between the larger distances.

This looks suspiciously like a modern piano keyboard, which of course, it is. The system is the same for all instruments of western civilization, but is clearly laid out on the keyboard instruments. This seems clear and simple, but actually took hundreds of years to finalize and still has some hidden flaws of tuning that professional musicians must deal with all the time. However, it can be noticed that a pattern can be created if you proceed from any pitch to its octave. Furthermore, as all of the pitches are considered, no two patterns are the same. Over time, two of the patterns became preferred, the one from **A** to **A** and the one from **C** to **C**. In these instances, either the **A** or **C** become the tonal center.

The pattern created when going from **A** to **A** is easily duplicated when going from **D** to **D** if only one small change is made: Instead of using the pitch **B**, use the pitch just to the left of **B**. The same pattern is created going from **E** to **E** if, instead of **F**, the key just to the right of **F** is used. Similarly, the pattern created when proceeding from **C** to **C** is duplicated when going from **F** to **F** if, again, the pitch just to the left of **B** is used instead of **B**. And, this pattern is recreated when going from **G** to **G** if the pitch just to the right of **F** is used.

Thus, with very small adjustments the two preferred patterns with their corresponding keytones, can be utilized on many pitches. In fact, the pattern can be duplicated starting on any pitch.

Atonality

atonal music
atonality

Music which lacks the feeling of a tonal center is known as **atonal music** and creates the comprehensive sense of **atonality**. Though almost all music of all Western styles is tonal music, composers of the twentieth century have produced many astounding musical experiences through the use of atonality. Because of the strong sense of unrest and insecurity felt in atonal music, it is a valuable tool for background music of dramas, tales of mystery and suspense, and Sci-Fi thrillers.

STRUCTURAL UNITS

Motive

motive

Often compared to a word in language — individual pitches instead of letters are combined to create a single image — the shortest possible complete melodic statement is known as a **motive**. The entire song POP GOES THE WEASEL is simply a melodic motive, two repetitions of the motive, then the "POP" and ending. Think about the motivic elements of songs like HAPPY BIRTHDAY TO YOU, WHEN THE SAINTS GO MARCHING IN, and SKIP TO MY LOU. The song ARE YOU SLEEPING is made of four clearly discernible independent motives, each repeated once. Of course, the most famous motive in the world is the four-note opening of Beethoven's Symphony No. 5.

repetition
imitation

Restating a musical motive exactly as previously heard is called, of course, **repetition**. Of course, the use of repetition is not limited to motives. Similarly, **imitation** is the identifiable mimicking of music. Imitation is often used between two or more instruments. Within a single melody, using one instrument, parts of a melody may be imitated within the melody itself. An example is MARY HAD A LITTLE LAMB, where the distinctive repetition of the rhythmic short-short-long on LIT-TLE-LAMB is imitated on different pitches.

sequence

If a short melodic motive is imitated three, four or more times in a predictable order, a **sequence** is formed. A good example of a sequence is heard in the Christmas carol ANGELS WE HAVE HEARD ON HIGH when the word Gloria is sung:

Glo – o – o – o – o – o – o – ri–a,   in Ex– cel–sis De – o

PHRASE

phrase
cadence

Often containing several of the unifying factors of motives, repetitions, imitations, and or sequences, a **phrase** is a longer musical statement ending with a cadence. A **cadence** is a pause or resting place. A musical phrase is often compared with a clause or phrase in language. The song ARE YOU SLEEPING consists of only one phrase. The song WHEN THE SAINTS GO MARCHING IN contains two phrases as does the song JINGLE BELLS. Notice that the two phrases of JINGLE BELLS start exactly the same. The phrases do not end the same, but they start identically. Two phrases that start the same are said to be **parallel phrases**.

parallel phrases

contrasting phrases

The two phrases of the song WHEN THE SAINTS GO MARCHING IN do not start the same. Two phrases that start differently are said to be **contrasting phrases**.

Let's do one more example for clarification: Consider the complete song HOME ON THE RANGE.

Oh, give me a home where the buffalo roam, where the deer and the antelope play,
Where seldom is heard a discouraging word, and the skies are not cloudy all day.
Home, home on the range where the deer and the antelope play,
Where seldom is heard a discouraging word, and the skies are not cloudy all day.

This song consists of four phrases. The first and second phrases are parallel. The third phrase is contrasting to the first two, but the last phrase is once again parallel to phrases one and two.

Listening Composition

SYMPHONY NO. 40, 1st mvt.
Classical Style Period

WOLFGANG AMADEUS MOZART
1756-1791

We know him as Wolfgang Amadeus Mozart. However, he was christened Joannes Chrysotomus Wolfgangus Theophilus Mozart in Salzburg, Austria. (The Greek "Theophilus," meaning "loved by God," is translated as "Gottlieb" in German and "Amadeus" in Latin.) By the age of five, the young Mozart was already an accomplished performer on the organ, violin, and harpsichord. Mozart's affinity toward music is no surprise — his father, Leopold, was a well-known violinist, and his sister, Marianne (also called Nanerl), was an outstanding harpsichordist — but his abilities, rightly described as "genius," were truly astounding.

Between 1762 and 1766, Leopold took his children on tour in an effort to present their remarkable talents to the world. They traveled to Munich, Augsburg, Mainz, Frankfurt, Brussels, Paris, Versailles, London, Amsterdam, Geneva, Berne, and Zurich. Three years later, they traveled to Italy, visiting Florence, Rome, Naples, Bologna, and Milan. Wherever they went, the children astonished the audiences of the royal courts. Young Wolfgang would often perform on the harpsichord with the keys covered by a cloth, improvise elaborately on a theme given to him on the spot, write compositions while locked in a room, and pass the strictest tests put upon him by the famous musicians of Europe.

As an adult, Mozart, besides music, enjoyed horseback riding (though he was always a little nervous) and dancing. He demonstrated a good sense of humor and a pleasant outlook, though the serious side of life was never lost. He was closely attached to and respectful of his strong-willed father, but was free enough to establish a family and an independent life in

69

Vienna. Mozart, having been prone to illness all of his life, died on December 5, 1791. The following are some of his letters:

To His Father
Vienna, April 8, 1781

My very dear father,

I began a lengthy and more interesting letter to you, but I wrote too much about Brunetti in it, and was afraid that his curiosity might tempt him to open the letter, because Ceccarelli is with me. I shall send it to you by the next post and in it shall write more fully than I can today. Meanwhile, you will have received my other letter. I told you about the applause in the theater, but I must add that what delighted and surprised me most of all was the amazing silence (and also the cries of "Bravo!") while I was playing. This is certainly honor enough in Vienna, where there are such numbers and numbers of good pianists. Today, we had a concert, where three of my compositions were performed — new ones, of course: a rondo for a concerto for Brunetti; a sonata with violin accompaniment for myself, which I composed last night between eleven and twelve (but in order to finish it, I only wrote out the accompaniment for Brunetti and retained my own part in my head); and then a rondo for Ceccarelli, which I had him repeat. I must now beg you to send me a letter as soon as you can to give me your fatherly and most friendly advice on the following matter. It is said that we are to return to Salzburg in two weeks. I can stay on here, and that not to my loss, but to my advantage. So, I am planning to ask the Archbishop to allow me to remain in Vienna. Dearest father, I love you dearly; that you must realize from the fact that for your sake I renounce all my wishes and desires. For, were it not for you, I swear on my honor that I should not pause for one moment to leave the Archbishop's service. I should give a grand concert, take four pupils, and in a year I should have got on so well in Vienna that I could make at least a thousand thalers a year. I assure you that I often find it difficult to throw away my fate as I am doing. As you say, I am still young. True, but to waste one's youth on inactivity in such an unpleasant place as Salzburg is really very sad. I should like to have your kind and fatherly advice about this, and very soon, for I must tell him what I am going to do. But do have confidence in me, for I am more sensible now. Farewell. I kiss your hands a thousand times and embrace my dear sister with all my heart and am ever your most obedient son.

W. A. Mozart

To His Father
Vienna, April 11, 1781

My very dear father,

Thank the Lord at last that coarse and dirty Brunetti has left. He is a disgrace to his master, to himself and to the whole orchestra — or so say Ceccarelli and I.

There is not a word of truth in all the Vienna news that you have heard, except that Ceccarelli is to sing in the opera at Venice during the next carnival. Great Heavens! A thousand demons! I hope that this is not swearing, for if so, I must at once go and confess again. For I have just returned from confession, because tomorrow the Archbishop in his sublime person is to feed the whole Court Personnel.

When I think that I must leave Vienna without bringing home at least a thousand gulden, my heart is hurting indeed. So, for the sake of a malevolent Prince who haunts me ever day and only pays me a lousy salary of four hundred gulden, I am to throw away a thousand? For I should absolutely make that sum if I were to give a concert. When we had our first grand concert in this house, the Archbishop sent each of us four ducats. At the last concert for which I composed a new rondo for Brunetti, a new sonata for myself, and also a new rondo for Ceccarelli, I received nothing. But what made me almost desperate was that the very same evening we had this disgusting concert, I was invited to Countess Thun's, but of course could not go; and who should be there but the Emperor Adamberger and Madame Weigl.

You have said that I must not forget you! That you rejoice to think that I do not, gives me the greatest pleasure. But if you could believe it possible that I should forget you, that indeed would pain me terribly. You say that I must recall that I have an immortal soul.

Not only do I think it, but I firmly believe it. Now farewell. I kiss your hands a thousand times and embrace my sister with all my heart and am ever your most obedient son.

W. A. Mozart

To His Father

Vienna, December 15, 1781

Dearest Father,

You demand an explanation of the words in the closing sentence of my last letter! Oh, how gladly would I have opened my heart to you long ago, but I was deterred by the reprimands you might have made to me for thinking of such a thing at an unseasonable time — although thinking can never be unseasonable. Meanwhile, I am very anxious to secure here a small but certain income, which, together with what chance may provide, will enable me to live here quite well — and then, to marry! You are horrified at the idea? But I beg you, dearest, most beloved Father, to listen to me. I have been obligated to reveal my plans to you. You should, therefore, allow me to inform you of my well-founded reasons. The voice of nature speaks as loud in me as to others, louder, perhaps, than in many a big strong lout of a fellow. I simply cannot live as most young men do in these days. In the first place, I have too much religion; in the second place, I have too great a love of my neighbor and too high a feeling of honor to seduce an innocent girl; and, in the third place, I have too much horror and disgust, too much fear and dread of diseases and too much care for my health to fool about with whores. So I can swear that I have never had relations of that sort with any woman. Besides, if such a thing had occurred, I should not have concealed it from you; for, after all, to err is natural enough in a man, and to err once would be mere weakness — although indeed I should not undertake to promise that if I had erred once in this way, I should stop short at one slip. However, I stake my life on the truth of what I have told you. I am aware that this reason, powerful as it is, is not enough. But owing to my disposition, which is more inclined to a peaceful and domestic existence than to revelry, I who from my youth up have never been accustomed to look after my own belongings, linen, clothes and so forth, cannot think of anything more necessary to me than a wife. I assure you that I am often obliged to spend unnecessarily, simply because I do not pay attention to things. I am absolutely convinced that I will manage better with a wife, than I do myself. And how many useless expenses would be avoided. True, other expenses would have to be met, but one knows what they are and can be prepared for them. In short, one leads a well-ordered existence. A bachelor, in my opinion, is only half alive. Such are my views and I cannot help but think this way. I have thought about this matter several times and reflected sufficiently, and I shall not change my mind.

But who is the object of my love? Do not be horrified again, I beg you. Surely not one of the Webers? Yes, one of the Webers, but not Josefa, nor Sophie, but Constanze, the middle one. In no other family have I ever met such differences of character. The eldest is a lazy, disloyal woman, and as cunning as a fox. Miss Lange is a false, malicious person and a coquette. The youngest is still too young to be anything in particular. She has a good disposition, but is a feather-headed creature. May God protect her from seduction! But the middle one, my good, dear Constanze, is the martyr of the family and, probably for that very reason, is the kindest-hearted, the cleverest, and in short, the best of them all. She makes herself responsible for the entire household and yet in their opinion she does nothing right. Oh, my most beloved father, I could fill whole pages with my descriptions of all the scenes that I have witnessed in that house. If you want to read them, I shall do so in my next letter.

Accordingly, all that I desire is to have a small assured income (of which, thank God, I have good hopes), and then I shall never cease entreating you to allow me to save this poor girl and to make myself and her and, if I might add, all of us very pleased. For surely, you are happy, when I am happy? And you are to enjoy one half of my fixed income. My dearest father, I have opened my heart to you and explained my words. It is now my turn to entreat you to explain yours in your last letter. You say that I cannot imagine that you were aware of a proposal which had been made to me and to which I, at the time when you heard of it, had not yet replied. I do not understand one word of this. I know of no such proposal. Please take heart on your son! I kiss your hands a thousand times and am ever your most obedient son.

W. A. Mozart

To His Father
Vienna, July 27, 1782

My very dear father,

Dearest, most beloved father, I implore you by all you hold dear in the world to give your consent to my marriage with my dear Constanze. Do not suppose that it is just for the sake of getting married. If that were my only intention, I would gladly wait. But I realize that it is absolutely necessary for my own honor and for that of my girl, and for the sake of my health and spirits. My heart is restless and my head confused. In such a state, how can one think and work to any good purpose? And why am I in this condition? Well, because most people think that we are already married. Her mother gets very much annoyed when she hears these rumors, and, as for the poor girl and myself, we are tormented to death. This state of affairs can be remedied so easily. Believe me, it is just as easy to live in expensive Vienna as anywhere else. It all depends on economy and good management, which cannot be expected from a young fellow, particularly if he is in love. Whoever gets a wife like my Constanze will certainly be a happy man. We intend to live very modestly and quietly, and yet we shall be happy. Do not be uneasy, for if I were to fail today, God forbid, I would bet that the leading nobles would stand by me manfully and the more so if I were married. I say this with full confidence. I know what Prince Kaunitz has said about me to the Emperor and the Archduke Maximilian. Most beloved father, I am longing to have your approval. I feel sure that you will give it, for my honor and my peace of mind depend upon it. Do not postpone too long the joy of embracing your son and his wife. I kiss your hands a thousand times and am ever your obedient son.

W. A. Mozart

To His Father
Vienna, August 7, 1782

My very dear father,

You are very wrong in your son if you can think him capable of acting dishonestly. My dear Constanze — now, thank God, at last my wife — knew my circumstances and heard from me long ago all that I had to expect from you. But her affection and her love for me were so great that she willingly and joyfully sacrificed her whole future to share my fate. I kiss your hands and thank you with all the love which a son has ever felt for a father, for your kind consent and fatherly blessing. But indeed, I could safely depend on it. For you know that I myself could but see only too clearly all the objections that could be raised against such a move. At the same time, you also know that I could not act otherwise, without hurting my conscience and my honor. Therefore, I could certainly depend on your consent. So it was that, having waited two post-days in vain for a response and the ceremony having been fixed for a day by which I was certain to have received it, I was married by the blessing of God to my beloved Constanze. I was very assured of your consent and was therefore comforted.

The following day I received your two letters at once. Well, it is over! I only ask your forgiveness for my hasty trust in your fatherly love. In this frank confession, you have clear proof of my love of truth and hatred of a lie. Next post-day, my dear wife will ask her dearest, most beloved father-in-law for his valued friendship. No one was present at the wedding save her mother and her youngest sister, Herr von Thorwart, as guardian and witness for both of us, Herr von Cetto, district councilman, who gave away the bride, and Gilowsky as my best man. When we had been joined together, both my wife and I began to weep. All present, even the priest, were deeply touched and all wept to see how much our hearts were moved. Our entire wedding feast consisted of a supper given for us by the Baroness von Walstadten, which was princely. My dear Constanze is now looking forward to a visit to Salzburg, and I know that you will rejoice in my joy when you get to know her, that is, if you agree with me that a right-minded, honest, virtuous, and amiable wife is a blessing to her husband.

I send you herewith a short march. I only hope that all will reach you in good time, and be to your taste. The first Allegro must be played with great fire, the last as fast as possible. My opera was given again yesterday at Gluck's request. He has been very complimentary to me about it. I am lunching with him tomorrow. You see by my writing how I must hurry. Good-bye. My dear wife and I kiss your hands a thousand times and we both embrace our dear sister with all our hearts and I am ever your most obedient son.

W. A. Mozart

To His Father
Vienna, April 4, 1787

My very dear father,

This very moment I have received a piece of news which greatly distresses me, the more so because I gathered from your last letter that, thank God, you were very well indeed. But now I hear that you are really ill. I need hardly tell you how much I am hoping to receive some reassuring news from you. And I still expect it, although I have now made a habit of being prepared in all affairs of life for the worst. As death, when we think about it closely, is the true goal of our life, I have formed during the last few years such close relations with this best and truest friend of mankind, that his image is not only no longer terrifying to me, but is indeed very soothing and comforting! And I thank God for graciously granting me the opportunity (you know what I mean) of learning that death is the key which unlocks the door to our true happiness. I never lie down at night without pondering that — young as I am — I may not live to see another day. Yet no one could say that I am glum or discontented. For this blessing I daily thank my Creator and wish with all my heart that each one of my fellow creatures could find the same satisfaction. In the letter which Madame Storace took away with her, I expressed my views to you on this issue, in connection with the sad death of my dearest and most beloved friend, the Count von Hatzfeld. He was just thirty-one, my own age. I do not feel sorry for him, but I pity most sincerely both myself and all who knew him well. But, if contrary to all expectations, you are not getting better, do not hide it from me. Tell me the whole truth or get someone to write it to me, so that as quickly as is humanly possible I may come to your arms. I entreat you by all that is sacred to both of us. Nevertheless, I trust that I shall soon have a reassuring letter from you, and cherishing this good hope, I and my wife and our little Karl kiss your hands a thousand times and I am ever your most obedient son.

W. A. Mozart

To His Wife
Dresden, April 13, 1789

Dearest, Most Beloved Little Wife,

We expected to reach Dresden after dinner on Saturday, but we did not arrive until yesterday, Sunday, at two o'clock in the afternoon, because the roads were so bad. All the same, I went yesterday to the Neumanns, where Madame Duschek is staying, in order to deliver her husband's letter. Her room is on the third floor beside the corridor and from it you can see anyone who is coming to the house. When I arrived at the door, Herr Neumann was already there and asked me to whom he had the honor of speaking. "I shall tell you in a moment," I replied, "but please do me the favor of calling Madame Duschek, so that my joke may not be ruined." But at the same moment Madame Duschek appeared, for she had recognized me from the window and had said, "Why here comes someone who looks like Mozart." Well, we all laughed.

Dearest little wife, if only I had a letter from you! If I were to tell you all the things I do with your dear portrait, I think that you would often laugh. For instance, when I take it out of its case, I say, "Good-day, little rascal, little turned-up nose, little bagatelle," and when I put it away again, I let it slip in very slowly, saying all the time, "Good night, little mouse, sleep well." Well, I suppose I have been writing something very foolish (to the world at all events); but to us who love each other so dearly, it is not foolish at all. Today is the sixth day since I left you and, by Heaven, it seems a year.

I know you will have some difficulty here and there in reading my letter, because I am writing in a hurry and therefore rather badly. Good-bye, my only love! The carriage is waiting. Farewell, and love me forever as I love you. I kiss you a million times most lovingly and am ever your husband who loves you tenderly.

W. A. Mozart

To His Wife
Vienna, October 8 & 9, 1791

Dearest, Most Beloved Little Wife,

I was extremely delighted and overjoyed to find your letter on my return from the opera. Although Saturday, as it is post-day, is always a bad night, the opera was performed to a full house and with the usual applause and repetition of numbers. It will be given again tomorrow, but there will be no performance on Monday.

At the opera everything was very pleasant and I stayed to the end. But during Papageno's aria with the glockenspiel I went behind the scenes; I felt an impulse today to play it myself. Well, just for excitement, at the point where Schikaneder has a pause, I played an arpeggio. He was startled, looked behind the wings and saw me. When he had his next pause, I played no arpeggio. This time he stopped and refused to go on. I guessed what he was thinking and again played a chord. He then struck the glockenspiel and said "Shut up." Whereupon everyone laughed. I am inclined to think that this joke taught many of the audience for the first time that Papageno does not play the instrument himself. By the way, you have no idea how charming the music sounds when you hear it from a box close to the orchestra. It sounds much better than from the gallery. As soon as you return, you must try this for yourself.

W. A. Mozart

Representative Composition

SYMPHONY NO. 40, 1st Mvt.

Type of Composition: **Movement from a symphony**

Structure: **Sonata Form.** Sonata form can be broken into three large parts with the names Exposition, Development, and Recapitulation. The exposition "exposes" the motives and main melodies (called themes) upon which the entire movement is built. Specifically, in the Exposition are two main themes presented and a closing theme (the closing theme is very similar to the opening theme). The Development section is like a series of variations on the material presented in the exposition. The Recapitulation restates the two main themes and the closing theme of the exposition. At the very end is added an ending (called a Coda).

TIME	LARGE STRUCTURE	INTERNAL STRUCTURE	COMMENTARY
0:00 (1:52)	**Exposition**	Theme 1	Strings begin Theme I which is built on a three-note motive. The direction of the motive is downward, as is the overall direction of the Theme.
0:23 (2:15)			Theme I begins again, but its continuation is changed slightly.
0:31 (2:23)			Loud chords interrupt Theme I, introducing a new ascending motive.
0:49 (2:41)		Theme II	The strings (assisted by the woodwinds) state Theme II. This melody is a contrast to Theme I. Instead of short, detached notes, the pitches are smoothly connected. The contour is downward.
0:58 (2:48)			Theme II is repeated. This time, however, the woodwinds lead the way, assisted by the strings.
1:10 (3:00)			A crescendo leads the smooth Theme II back toward the detached notes indicative of Theme I.
1:21 (3:12)		Closing Theme	The three-note motive of Theme I is stated, repeated, and imitated by the woodwinds, then the strings, ending with fast downward passages at a loud dynamic level.
1:52	THE EXPOSITION IS REPEATED (See times in parentheses.)		

3:35	**Development**		The development begins as a continuation of the ending of the Exposition. Then, the woodwinds begin a descending line reminiscent of Theme II, overlapped by a sequence built on the first part of Theme I played by the violins.
4:00			The sequence is interrupted as the lower strings play Theme I while the violins, playing new sequences, woodwinds, and French horns combined in a vigorous polyphonic texture.
4:26			A soft ascending sequence built on the motive of Theme I is played by the violins while woodwinds answer. Melodic statements become shorter in length (descending sequences built on the main motive).
4:43			Sudden loud, short, inverted statements of the main motive by strings while woodwinds play vigorous, disjunct statements. Polyphonic texture.
4:51			Woodwinds continue polyphonic texture softly.
4:57	**Recapitulation**	Theme I	
6:06		Theme II	
6:44		Closing Theme	
7:06		Coda	The Coda is introduced through loud, ascending, syncopated chords by the woodwinds. Violins repeat the main motive. Loud, homophonic chords lead to the end.

Chapter 6

HARMONY AND TEXTURE

HARMONY

Melody, with pitches following each other in succession, is often referred to as the horizontal aspect of music. If this be the case, harmony (pitches heard simultaneously) would then be the vertical. Harmony is most often used to form accompaniments to melodies. These may be the simple strumming of guitar chords when singing popular songs, the blending of voices in a barbershop quartet, the use of piano and organ with a church choir, or the elaborate combinations of sounds of a larger orchestra. But harmony serves a greater function than simply accompanying melody. The type of harmony chosen can powerfully change the emotion of a song or the entire character of a large composition. Effects of seriousness, melancholy, suspense, romance, etc. can be produced by harmony.

Types of Harmony

consonant harmony
consonance
dissonant harmony
dissonance

When two pitches are heard together, there is generally one of two responses. The sound will produce either a feeling of stability or a feeling of instability. Harmony with a sensation of stability and the absence of tension is called **consonant harmony** or simply **consonance**. Conversely, the feeling of instability and tension is **dissonant harmony** or **dissonance**. Dissonance is often described as a clashing of pitches whereas consonance produces what most people consider a less-shocking blend of sounds. The clash felt when hearing dissonance is the result of the ear drum trying to sort out and adjust to sound waves which are different, but which are only *slightly* different. Consider the following: Looking at the pitches, it can be seen that they can be combined with others, either nearby (similar vibrations) or far away (less similar vibrations).

A B C D E F G A

The pitch **A** combined with a **B** or a **G** will produce a dissonant sound.

A B C D E F G A

An **A** combined with a **D** or an **E** will produce a consonant sound.

A B C D E F G A

triad

The pitch **A** combined with a **C** or **F** is presently considered a consonant sound, but in the past it was considered dissonant and still recognized by musicians as less stable (stability = consonance) than the combination of **A** with **D** or **E**. However, in today's most commonly heard music, a combination such as pitch **A** with **E** is not generally heard without the other consonant pitch **C** also present. The sound created by three pitches in this relationship form what is known as a **triad**. A **chord** may be defined as the simultaneous sounding of three or more pitches, but the chords most widely used are all based on triads.

Functional Harmony

As indicated previously, the patterns used for the melodies of the most commonly heard music creates tonal music.

The harmonic support of this music, built on chords formed by triads, also serves to direct the listener toward a key

functional harmony

center. The harmony has a utilitarian purpose and is thus called **functional harmony**.

Again, as was described in the analysis of melody, music is most interesting when tension and release are involved. Establishing a tonal center, moving away from it, then back, is an example of this. Let's consider the function of harmony in this process. In the key of C, triads could be formed on each pitch used:

C-E-G

D-F-A

E-G-B

F-A-C

G-B-D

A-C-E

B-D-F

The triad built on the keytone **C** is, of course, consonant and stable. Now, considering the most dissonant pitches with the pitch **C** are **D** and **B**. Only two triads, **G-B-D** and **B-D-F**, contain both these dissonant pitches. These triads, when used in supplying harmony, create great tension, and therefore, there is a great sense of resolution when the sound resolves back to the **C** triad. Often, the triad **G-B-D** is combined with **B-D-F** to form the chord **G-B-D-F**. This chord strongly directs the listener to desire a return to the tonal center. This example is only one of many devices used in the functional role of harmony. All are for the enrichment of music and the musical experience.

TEXTURE

texture

The word texture is from a Latin word meaning "to weave together." Thus, the various ways in which musical sounds are woven together is called the **texture**. And, just as the word textile means *fabric*, texture in music is often referred to as the musical fabric. This fabric can be analyzed with general concepts such as thick, thin, heavy, and light, or can be analyzed by the more specific musical terms of monophonic, homophonic or polyphonic.

Monophony

Just as a piece of cloth begins with a single thread, a single melody line, without harmonic support or accompaniment, is the beginning of the study of texture. This type of texture is known as **monophony**, creating a **monophonic texture**. A person singing alone creates a monophonic texture, as does a lone trumpet player. However, a monophonic texture is also created by several persons singing or several trumpets playing if, and only if, the musicians are all producing the same melody at the same time and if there is no harmony involved. Similarly, since the distance of an octave is not recognized as creating harmony, the production of a single unaccompanied melody in octaves is considered monophonic.

monophony
monophonic texture

Homophony

The most common presentation of a melody is with added harmony or harmonic accompaniment. These create **homophony**. The pitches harmonizing a melody may be sounded simultaneously with the melody so that they are not recognized as distinct from it, or they may be organized rhythmically independent of the melody. Both create the **homophonic texture** as long as the melody is clearly presented as the more important.

homophony

homophonic texture

Polyphony

When two or more melodies of relatively equal importance are heard at the same time, the result is **polyphony**. Synonymous with the terms polyphony and **polyphonic texture** are **counterpoint** and **contrapuntal texture**. Examples of

polyphony
polyphonic texture
counterpoint
contrapuntal texture

polyphony range from simply embellishing a melody with a countermelody to the complex sound of simultaneous improvising by the members of a Dixieland band. In these two examples, each of the independent melodies would be completely different. But a polyphonic texture is also created when one melody is performed in a manner so that the melody overlaps itself. For example, in a round such as ROW ROW ROW YOUR BOAT, one person may begin the song and another may enter a short time later. The intertwining melodic lines create the polyphonic texture.

As with any aspect of life, variety makes it more interesting. Knowing this, composers will freely change from one texture to another or vary the degree of density and weight in order to enhance the musical experience.

Listening Composition

SYMPHONY NO. 5, 1st mvt.
Romantic Style Period

LUDWIG VAN BEETHOVEN
1770-1827

Ludwig van Beethoven was born in 1770 in Bonn, Germany. He began studying the violin at the age of five. His father, a singer, encouraged Beethoven to practice continually, wanting him to become a child prodigy like Mozart had been. By the age of nine, Beethoven was playing the piano and the organ.

Beethoven's abilities attracted the attention of Maximilian Franz, the brother of the German emperor Josef II. Franz assisted him in visiting Vienna, the European center of culture and musical training, in 1787. There, Beethoven was able to meet Mozart, who recognized Beethoven's talent and predicted that he would make a great impression on the world some day.

During this visit, Beethoven may have had a few lessons in composition with Mozart, but by the time Beethoven settled permanently in Vienna in 1792, Mozart had already died. However, in that city, Beethoven studied with great teachers, including Franz Joseph Haydn, Johann Schenk, and Antonio Salieri.

Around the age of 25, Beethoven began to lose his hearing, becoming completely deaf by 1819. Though Beethoven was tremendously emotionally affected by his deafness, he continued to compose great works. Upon his death in 1827, 20,000 people attended his funeral. The following are some of his letters, and writings about him by acquaintances:

To Carl Amenda
Vienna, June 1, 1800

My dear, my good Amenda, my heartily beloved friend,

With deep feelings, with a mixture of pain and pleasure did I receive and read your last letter. How can I compare your fidelity, your attachment to me? Oh, how wonderful it is that you are so kind to me. Yes, I realize that you, of all men, are the most trustworthy. You are no Viennese friend. No, you are like those such my native country produces. How frequently do I wish you were with me, for your Beethoven is very unhappy and at strife with nature and Creator. The latter I have often cursed for exposing His creatures to situations in which the richest buds are crushed and destroyed. Only think that the noblest part of me, my sense of hearing, has become weaker. Already when you were with me I noticed traces of the problem, but I did not mention it. Now it has become worse, and it remains to be seen whether it can ever be cured. The main cause of it is the condition of my bowels. So far as this is concerned, I am almost well, but I greatly fear that my hearing will not get better. Maladies of this sort are the most difficult of all to heal. What a sad life I am now compelled to lead. I must stay away from all that is near and dear to me.

To Dr. F. Wegeler
Vienna, June 29, 1800

Dear Wegeler,

I am most grateful to you for thinking of me. You are so very kind, and are not held back by anything, not even by my inexcusable negligence, but always remain a faithful, good, and honest friend. I could never forget you, and especially all of you who were so good and affectionate to me. There are moments in which I myself long for you — yes, and wish to spend more time with you. My native land, the beautiful country in which I first saw the light of the world, is as pretty and distinct before my eyes as when I left you. In short,

I shall again greet our father Rhine. When that will be I cannot tell yet. I will tell you this much, that you shall find me better, more perfect, and if in our native land there are any signals of returning prosperity, I will only use my art for the benefit of the poor.

You are interested in knowing something about my present condition. Well, at the moment it is not too bad. Since last year, Lichnowsky, who, however incredible it may appear when I relate it to you, was always my warmest friend, and has remained so (of course there have been slight misunderstandings between us, but these have only made our friendship stronger), has settled a fixed sum of 600 florins on me, and I can draw on it so long as I fail to find a suitable post. My compositions are bringing in a moderate sum, and, I might add that it is difficult for me to fill the requests for new compositions that I have received. Also, for every work I have six, seven or more publishers. They do not bargain with me. I demand and they pay. You see how wonderful it is. Also I am more frugal than I used to be. If I should settle here, I shall certainly contrive to get one day every year for concerts, of which I have already given some.

Only my envious demon, my illness, has thrown obstacles in my way. For example, my hearing has become weaker during the last three years. Frank wanted to restore me to health by means of strengthening medicines, and to cure my deafness by means of almond oils, but nothing came of these remedies. My hearing only became worse.

I really lead a wretched life, for nearly two years I have been avoiding almost all my friends, because I simply cannot tell people that I am deaf. If I had any other occupation it would be easier, but in my profession it is terrible. And as for my enemies — of whom I have no small number — what would they think about it? If I am at a certain distance from instruments or singers, I cannot hear the high notes. In conversation it is remarkable that there remains several people who have never noticed it. I am usually absent-minded, and they put it down to that. Moreover, I can often scarcely hear a person who speaks in a low tone. The tone, yes, but not the words. What will happen now, heaven knows. Vering says there will certainly be an improvement, if not a complete recovery. Frequently already I have cursed my life: Plutarch has been teaching me resignation. If it proves otherwise, I shall brave my fate, that at times I shall be the most depressed of God's creatures. What a miserable refuge, yet that is all that is left for me.

From the diary of Sir George Smart

Friday, September 9, 1825

At noon I took Ries to the hotel Wildemann, the lodgings of Mr. Schlesinger, the music-seller of Paris, as I gathered from Mr. Holz that Beethoven would be there, and there I did find him. He received me in the most flattering manner. There was a gathering of professors to hear Beethoven's new quartet, bought by Mr. Schlesinger. This quartet is three-quarters of an hour long. They performed it twice. It is very chromatic and there is a slow movement entitled, "Praise for the recovery of an invalid." Beethoven intended to allude to himself I suppose, for he was very ill during the early part of this year. He directed the performers, and took off his coat, the room being very warm and crowded. A staccato passage, not being expressed to the satisfaction of his sight, for alas, he could not hear, he seized Holz's violin and played the passage a quarter of a tone too flat.

Sunday, September 11

We had a most excellent dinner, toasts were given in the English style. Beethoven was delightfully gay but hurt that in the letter that Moscheles gave me his name was mixed up with the other professors. However, he got over it soon. He was very pleased and really surprised to see in the oratorio announcement I gave him that the "Mount of Olives" and his "Battle Symphony" were both performed the same evening.

After dinner he was coaxed to improvise on the piano. He played for about twenty minutes in a most extraordinary manner, sometimes very fortissimo, but full of creativity. When he arose at the end of his performance, he appeared greatly exhausted. No one could be more agreeable than he was — full of jokes. We all wrote to him by turns, but he can hear a little if you shout quite close to his left ear.

90

From the Autobiography of Louis Spohr

As, at the time when I made his acquaintance, Beethoven had ceased to perform either in public or at private gatherings, I was only given one opportunity to hear him, when by chance I went to see him during the rehearsal of a new trio. It was hardly an enjoyable experience because, to begin with, the piano was badly out of tune, a circumstance which did not trouble Beethoven as he could not hear the music, and secondly scarcely anything remained of the artist's once so greatly admired virtuosity, also because of his deafness. In the forte passages, the struggling deaf man struck the instrument with such violence that the strings rattled, while in the piano passages he played so softly that whole bars were inaudible and the music became difficult to understand, unless one were able to follow the pianoforte part in the manuscript. I was overcome with a feeling of great sorrow when I considered this hard fate of his. If it is a great misfortune for anyone to be deaf, how can a musician endure it without despairing? Beethoven's chronic melancholia no longer puzzled me.

To Frau Nanette Streicher
1816

I thank you for your interest in me. Matters are already improved. I have endured much today from Nany, but have thrown half a dozen books at her head as a New Year's gift.

So far as Baberi is concerned, she goes off early on Monday, so the other can also come in either in the afternoon about 2 o'clock or 3 o'clock whichever you think best. Nany asked me today whether Baberi was going to quit. I said no, she could at latest remain until Monday. For the rest I have reason to believe that Nany has been snooping around your house. The evening before last, Nany began to jeer at me for ringing the bell, after the manner of all low people, so she already knew that I had written you about her.

Yesterday her infernal tricks started again. I made short work of it, and threw at her my heavy chair which stands by the bed. I can't say much for Nany's honesty.

As soon as the new maid arrives, I will, the first time you pay me a visit, call her in, and in your presence express my doubts about the kitchen book. We shall see how matters go on, but usually when anything has happened between masters and servants, it is not any good after that. I beg you so to instruct the kitchen maid about to enter my service that she must take sides with you and me against Nany. For that purpose I will often write something which the other one does not need to know about. Besides, she may not be so greedy as Nany and Baberl. In short, the kitchen maid must always be in opposition to Nany. I assure you that what I have experienced with Nany exceeds the behavior of many servants I have had. I have strictly forbidden Nany to have strange visitors. And now goodbye.

In haste, your friend,
Beethoven

To Frau Nanette Streicher
1816

The criminal received her sentence today. She behaved almost like Caesar under the dagger, only with the difference, that in the first case there was truth at bottom, but hers was hopeless treason. The kitchen maid appears more capable than the other one. She keeps quite out of sight, a sign that she does not expect a good character reference, which, however, I had thought of giving her. Now I want a new housekeeper. I beg you, however, to think over what is best — common sense, and at the same time be sufficiently careful of our money. The new kitchen maid made an ugly face when asked to carry up wood, but I hope she will remember that our Saviour dragged His cross to Golgotha. I shall probably see you tomorrow.

In haste, your friend,
Beethoven

To Herr Zmeskall
1817

My Dear Good Zmeskall

I shall see you soon again in town. What is the right price for the repairing of boots? I have to pay my servant for this, who is always running about wearing his out.

92

I am really depressed at being condemned by my defective hearing to pass the greater part of my life with this most odious class of people, and to be in some degree dependent on them. Tomorrow, early, my servant will call on you. Please send me back a sealed answer.

I heard of your indisposition with great regret. As for me, I am often in despair, and almost tempted to end my life, for all these remedies produce no results. May God have compassion on me, for I look at myself as being lost!

I have a great deal to say to you. That this servant is a thief, I cannot doubt. He must be sent away. My health requires living at home and in greater comfort. If my condition does not change, I shall probably be in my grave. I thank God that the thread of my life will soon be spun out.

In haste, your friend,
Beethoven

Representative Composition

SYMPHONY NO. 5, 1st Mvt.

Type of Composition: **Movement from a symphony**

Structure: **Sonata Form.** Beethoven uses the classical sonata form consisting of Exposition, Development, and Recapitulation. However, many ideas established by Haydn and Mozart have been greatly expanded. For examples: The orchestra is larger and there is more independence of the instruments, allowing them to take advantage of their individual colors and technical abilities. The development section is longer and more elaborate. There are wider variations of expression (notice the dynamic range overall, the use of crescendos and decrescendos, and the "rubato" oboe solo before the Recapitulation). The coda is longer and more elaborate than in Mozart's Symphony No. 40, 1st Mvt.

TIME	LARGE STRUCTURE	INTERNAL STRUCTURE	COMMENTARY
0:00 (1:28)	**Exposition**	Theme I	The famous four-note motive, played by strings and clarinet, is introduced at a fortissimo dynamic level, utilizing the

		orchestra playing in unison and octave (thus, the texture is monophonic).
0:07 (1:34)		The dynamic level drops to piano as the motive is used to create a dialogue between the string instruments. The texture is polyphonic.
0:13 (1:39)		A crescendo leads to a forte level, then a suspension of the action occurs as the violins alone sustain a tone by means of a fermata.
0:19 (1:45)		The motive is stated in unison and octaves (as at the beginning), but on this occasion the statement occurs only once. Then, beginning at a piano dynamic level, a crescendo eventually takes the level to fortissimo.
0:44 (2:10)		French horns, playing in unison, state the motive (slightly altered) alone (monophonic texture), but extend the musical thought from four notes into a six-note phrase (this phrase will be developed later by Beethoven). The horns articulate in legato style which serves as an introduction to the second theme.
0:47 (2:13)	Theme II	The second theme is a contrast to the first. It is lyrical and legato. Although there is dialogue between violins, clarinets and flutes, the clearly-defined melody creates an homophonic texture.
1:09 (2:34)		An ending for Theme II, built on sequences, begins to return to the detached, quick notes associated with the original motive. This serves as an introduction to the Closing Theme.
1:18 (2:43)	Closing Theme	The Closing Theme is not made of new musical material, but utilizes the original four-note motive.

1:28   THE EXPOSITION IS REPEATED (See times in parentheses.)

2:54   **Development**

After two statements of the original four-note motive, a fermata introduces the Development section. The motive then continues to be used as a basis for dialogue between instruments. The polyphonic texture becomes thicker as French horns interrupt a melodic sequence begun by the violins.

2:57

The dialogue between instruments continues as the contra basses join the orchestra and the violins change the direction of the motive from descending to ascending. Other instruments (violas, cellos, bassoons, flutes and clarinets), however, struggle to maintain the downward direction. The battle is won by the violins as the other instruments play an altered, ascending form of the motive.

3:16

A crescendo leads to a series of repeated chords using the rhythm of the four-note motive. But the four notes soon become only three.

3:29

The legato theme, which had been introduced by the French horns in the exposition just before Theme II, now becomes the dominant melody. It is accompanied by the three-note rhythm just previously established.

3:39

A new two-note motive, derived from the middle of the legato theme just heard, becomes the foundation for a dialogue between strings and woodwinds. The two notes are eventually shortened to one note, allowing Beethoven to utilize essentially a one-note motive at a pianissimo dynamic level, although interrupted at one point by the fortissimo statement of the complete musical thought from where this material was taken.

3:59			The full orchestra again interrupts the pianissimo with a fortissimo statement of the original motive which leads to the recapitulation.
4:13	**Recapitulation**	Theme 1	The use of fermatas with the original motive mark the beginning of the Recapitulation. As at the beginning, the motive is used in polyphonic fashion until the action is suspended by means of a fermata. This time, however, the pitch being held is done so by the oboe instead of the violin. The oboe then, in monophonic texture, utilizes rubato to extend the musical thought, ending with another fermata. The dialogue between the instruments then continues. The introduction to the second theme is played this time by the bassoons instead of by the French horns.
5:03		Theme II	Theme II is stated. A crescendo from piano to fortissimo, sequences, and repeated chords leads to the Closing Theme.
5:37		Closing Theme	The Closing Theme, as before, uses the original four-note motive.
5:46		Coda	The four-note rhythm continues, but the pitches of the motive, instead of descending, stay the same, dramatically repeating a single chord. The Coda becomes more than an ending. It turns into a new development section, allowing even the introduction of new thematic material. A fermata suspends the action, then the original motive resumes at a pianissimo level. The full orchestra, at the level of fortissimo, then states a form of the four-note motive to bring the movement to a close.

Chapter 7

MUSICAL EXPRESSION

Pitches, rhythms, harmony. These mean nothing without an answer to the questions: What mood, feeling, image, or emotion is trying to be conveyed? Is the music to be light, happy, playful, heavy, serious, sad, melancholy, pensive, or meditative? Some answers to these questions may be indicated by the composer by means of notations on the music page, but, just as the power of the lines of a great speech depend on the orator, so too the message of the music rests on the shoulders of the performer. Elements of expression are needed in order to send mere vibrations on a journey to the inward planes of the soul. This concept is well presented in the words of musician and writer Johann Quantz in 1752:

> *No less must good execution be varied. Light and shadow must constantly be maintained. No listener will be moved by someone who always produces the notes with the same force or weakness and, so to speak, plays always in the same color. Good execution must be expressive and appropriate to each passion that one encounters. Only in this manner will he do justice to the intentions of the composer and to the ideas he had in mind when he wrote the piece. Your principal goal must always be the expression and sentiment of the piece. Accordingly, those who wish to maintain their supremacy over the machine, and wish to touch people, must play each piece with its proper fire.*

When writing the music, the composer does have certain control over expression. An example is the choice of instruments to be used. A brass quartet playing a composition will certainly carry a different emotional message than a string quartet playing the same composition. Similarly, the composer's expressive wishes as seen in the choices of harmony, phrasing, and contour are easily identifiable. However, the performer is often given great latitude in using the tools identified below for musical expression.

Articulation

articulation

staccato
legato
accent

Articulation is the manner in which pitches are started, sustained, and stopped. A series of short, detached pitches has the articulation of **staccato**. Pitches smoothly connected together are being presented in **legato** fashion. Placing an **accent** on a given pitch means giving special emphasis to the pitch. This may be accomplished by playing the pitch softer than other pitches, or by changing the articulation from staccato to legato, or vice versa. In the song POP GOES THE WEASEL the accent on the word *Pop* is created by a combination of loudness and the fact that that pitch is much higher than the surrounding pitches.

Round and round the mulberry bush the monkey chased the weasel,

The monkey thought 'twas all in fun, **POP** goes the weasel.

Also, try singing POP GOES THE WEASEL with staccato articulation, then legato.

Ornamentation

ornamentation
vibrato

Like a Christmas tree with lights, tinsel, and colorful balls, music can also be decorated. Three common devices for musical embellishment, **ornamentation**, are *vibrato, trills,* and *grace notes.* **Vibrato** is the slight wavering of a pitch. A violinist can generally be seen rapidly moving the left hand and wrist while playing. This motion, in turn, causes the pitch being played to waver.

Vibrato can be produced on most musical instruments. Piano, pipe organ, and percussion instruments are exceptions. Flute players and singers produce vibrato by means of quick pulsations of the diaphragm. Saxophone players generally increase and decrease pressure on the reed. Brass players can shake the horn or slightly move the jaw as they play. It is interesting that the common practice in a symphony orchestra is for the strings and flutes to use vibrato, while the clarinets, oboes, and bassoons do not. Brass players in a symphony will not use vibrato unless performing as a soloist, but in a jazz ensemble they always play with vibrato.

trill

A **trill** is the rapid alternation between two nearby pitches. Trills are commonly heard from flutes, violins, and other instruments of high pitch (as they imitate birds, for example), but are not common on instruments in the low pitch range unless the instrument is being heard in a solo capacity. On instruments with keys or valves, and on the string instruments, it is easy to execute a trill. But it is not so easy to produce a trill with the human voice. However, trained singers develop the ability to rapidly alternate between two pitches, sometimes with amazing facility — a remarkable feat.

grace note

A **grace note** is a pitch very briefly sounded, quickly moving to a nearby emphasized pitch. To get an idea of the sound of a grace note, try making the sound of a snare drum in a marching band: Dee-UMP, Dee-UMP, Dee-UMP UMP UMP. The *Dee's* are the grace notes.

The purpose of the grace note is to bring attention to the neighboring note. Now let's see how confusing we can be: Since the word *grace* means *special favor*, the grace note should really be the second pitch heard, not the first, because the second pitch is the one receiving the special attention!

Dynamics

dynamics

The word **dynamics** refers to the degree of loudness or softness in music. Italian terms are used to express dynamic levels, as indicated below:

pianissimo	very soft
piano	soft
mezzo piano	medium soft
mezzo forte	medium loud
forte	loud
fortissimo	very loud

terraced dynamics

crescendo
decrescendo

Changes in dynamics may be made by means of sudden shifts from one level to another, called **terraced dynamics**, or by gradual means. Gradually moving from one dynamic level to a louder level is accomplished through the use of a **crescendo**. Gradually getting softer utilizes a **decrescendo**.

When discussing dynamics, it must be remembered that loudness and softness are always relative terms. Points to ponder: 1) A fortissimo on a low pitch on a flute is about the same as the piano level of a trumpet. 2) In popular parlance, *crescendo* is sometimes synonymous with *loud*. ("The argument reached a crescendo, then the fight started!") Not so in music. A crescendo may be used to move from the level of pianissimo to piano.

A concluding remark on musical expression is found in the words of Thomas Mace, writing to music students in 1676:

> You will do well to remember to play loud and soft, sometimes briskly and sometimes gently and smoothly, here and there, as your fancy will prompt you. Many drudge and take pains to play their lessons very perfectly, as they call it, which, when they do, you will perceive little life or spirit in them. They do not labor to find out the humor, life, or spirit in their lessons.

Listening Composition

THE ERLKING
Romantic Style Period

FRANZ SCHUBERT
1797-1828

Born near Vienna, Austria, Franz Schubert is considered one of the greatest composers of the 19th century. He began violin and piano lessons when he was very young. At the age of 11, Schubert was admitted to the Vienna Court Choir, where he studied and trained for five years. During this time, he began composing songs and piano works.

Schubert's father was a schoolmaster, and Schubert originally planned to become an elementary school teacher. While training for this vocation, he took a position at his father's school. But he found teaching to be burdensome because it interfered with his desire to compose constantly. At one point, Schubert remarked, "I have come into the world for no other purpose than to compose."

To describe Franz Schubert as a "prolific" composer would be an understatement. Schubert went so far as to go to bed with his glasses on so that he could begin composing as soon as he awoke. In 1815 alone, he composed 144 songs; the next year, he composed 179 works, including an opera, a mass, and two symphonies. He gave up teaching at the age of 21 to devote himself entirely to his music. Before his death at a tragically young age, Schubert had written almost 1,000 pieces of music.

The speed at which Schubert composed was witnessed by a friend of his who saw the eighteen-year-old reading a poem entitled *The Erlking* by Göethe. Schubert held the book in his hands, and paced the floor several times. Then, "Suddenly he sat down, and in no time at all — just as quickly as he could write — there was a glorious ballad finished on the paper."

In 1817, Schubert submitted *The Erlking* to a publisher. It was rejected, and the manuscript was mistakenly returned to another songwriter named Francois Schubert, who lived in Dresden. Even though this particular piece is considered one of Schubert's best songs, it is apparent that the publisher and the Dresden *Schubert* did not think so. This is what Francois Schubert wrote to the publisher:

> *I received your esteemed letter enclosing a manuscript, to my astonishment, purported to be by me. I can assure you that I never composed this cantata. I will keep it in my custody in order to find out, if possible, who was so uncivil as to send you such wretched stuff, and also who is the fellow who takes my name in vain.*

Franz Peter Schubert was not very well known outside of Vienna during his lifetime, in part because he was shy. He rarely left his hometown. He was not a concert performer or conductor, nor did he teach music. He had no regular employment, and could not afford to rent a room on his own. His existence depended on the support of his friends, who were mostly writers and artists, and the occasional sale of a composition. It was for these friends that Schubert wrote and performed most of his music.

Schubert was destitute in 1812 when he wrote to his brother:

> How *would it be if you were to send me a few shillings a month? You would not even feel it . . . I base myself on the words of the Apostle Matthew, who also says, 'He that has two cloaks, let him give one to the poor,' etc. Meanwhile, I hope you will listen to the voice, which is ceaselessly calling on you, of your affectionate, impoverished, hopeful and - I repeat — impoverished brother,* Franz.

Sometime around age 25. Schubert, in the words of his friends, was led astray by a man named Franz Schober. Among the prostitutes of Vienna, Schubert contracted syphilis. It took six years for the disease to finally kill him at the age of thirty-one. During that long period, though he was ill and depressed, Schubert continued to compose, even taking a lesson in counterpoint from another musician during the last week of his life. His final request was to be buried near his idol, Ludwig van Beethoven, whom he greatly admired but was too shy to seek out.

Representative Composition

THE ERLKING

Type of Composition: **Art Song**

Structure: Freely composed song for voice and piano, unified by recurring motivic figures, symmetrical phrases, and rapid repeating notes in the accompaniment.

Commentary: In this song, the singer takes on the role of four characters: the narrator, the father, the young boy, and the Erlking (the specter of Death). The fast repeated notes of the piano throughout the piece represent not only the running horse on which the father and the boy are riding, but also the tension and urgency of trying to escape from the Erlking. To create the image of each character, it can be noted that Schubert used a medium range of pitches for the narrator, a low range for the father, and a high range for the boy. The range given to the Erlking is also high, the melodies that are "light" and "lyrical" (the Erlking is tempting the boy to come with him). Near the very end, a ritardando and decrescendo (to pianissimo) bring the song to the final words. The words "was dead" are presented in a very low pitch range and with a monophonic texture.

TIME	VOICE	GERMAN	ENGLISH
0:00	Piano Introduction		
0:25	Narrator	Wer reitet so spät durch Nacht und Wind? Es ist der Vater mit seinem Kind. Er hat den Knaben wohl in dem Arm. Er fasst ihn sicher; er hält ihn warm.	Who rides so late through night and wind? It is a father with his child. He has the boy close in his arms. He holds him tightly; he keeps him warm.
1:00	Father	Mein Sohn, was birgst du so bang dein Gesicht?	My son, why are you hiding your face so fearfully?
1:10	Son	Siehst, Vater, du den Erlkönig nicht? Den Erlenkönig mit Kron' und Schweif?	Don't you see the Erlking, father? The Erlking with his crown and his train?
1:28	Father	Mein Sohn, es ist ein Nebelstreif.	My son, it's only the mist.
1:40	Erlking	Du liebes Kind, komm, geh mit mir! Gar schöne Spiele Spiel' ich mit dir. Manch bunte Blumen sind an dem Strand. Meine Mutter hat manch gülden Gewand.	My lovely child, come, go with me. I'll play beautiful games with you. Many colorful flowers are on the shore. My mother has many golden robes.
2:05	Son	Mein Vater, mein Vater, und hörest du nicht was Erlenkönig mir leise verspricht?	My father, my father, and don't you hear what the Erlking is whispering to me?
2:20	Father	Sei ruhig, bleibe ruhig, mein Kind; in dürren, Blättern säuselt der Wind.	Be quiet, stay quiet, my son, the dead leaaves are rustled by the wind.
2:30	Erlking	Willst, feiner Knabe, du mit mir gehn? Meine Töchter sollen dich warten schön; meine Töchter führen den nächtlichen Reihn und Wiegen und tanzen und singen dich ein.	Will you come with me, handsome boy? My daughters will wait upon you; my daughters lead the nightly dancing and will rock and dance and sing you to sleep.
2:50	Son	Mein Vater, mein Vater, und siehst du nicht dort Erlkönigs Töchter am düstern Ort?	My father, my father, and don't you see the Erlking's daughter over there in the darkness?

3:05	Father	Mein Sohn, mein Sohn, ich seh es genau. Es scheinen die alten Weiden so grau.	My son, my son, I see it clearly. It is the shining of the old gray willows.
3:25	Erlking	Ich liebe dich, mich reizt deine schöne Gestalt, und bist du nicht willig, so brauch ich Gewalt.	I love you, your beautiful figure pleases me, and if you are not willing, I will use force.
3:37	Son	Mein Vater, mein Vater, jetzt fasst er mich an! Erlkönig hat mir ein Leids gethan!	My father, my father, now he has taken hold of me! The Erlking has hurt me!
3:52	Narrator	Dem Vater grauset's, er reitet geschwind. Er hält in den Armen das ächzende Kind. Erreicht den Hof mit Müh und Noth. In seinen Armen das Kind war tot.	The father shudders, he rides on in haste. He holds the sobbing child in his arms. He reaches the courtyard in misery and distress. In his arms, the child was dead.

PART II

HISTORICAL PERSPECTIVES

Chapter 8

MUSIC STYLE PERIODS

It is interesting that while any given member of a society is an individual and free to think and act independently, people in a society tend to move through time as a recognizable entity, approaching the many areas of life in a similar manner and with a similar thought process. As an example, consider the relatively recent history of the United States. Following World War II, the country had a focus on structure and discipline. In education, heavy emphasis was placed on science and mathematics. The people of the U.S. were concerned with the defeat of communism and being the world leader in space exploration. Patriotism was very high. Then, in the late 1950's and through the 1960's a different way of viewing life emerged. Questioning of and rebellion against the status quo can be seen in the acceptance of previously unacceptable gyrations as demonstrated by Elvis, racial marches and riots, violent demonstrations and protests of the Vietnam War, LSD, the idealizing of four long-haired boys from Liverpool, and an education system that stressed feelings and self above reading, multiplication tables, and courtesy to others.

During these decades, all people of the United States, of course, did not think the same. During the 1950's some were striving for change even while the majority conformed to the norm. But, when the norm changed in the 1960's, movements began to draw the country into a more *back to basics* society — which happened in the late 1970's and 80's.

All this is being said to draw attention to a *society moving as a society*. But this small time period doesn't paint the complete picture. If our society were analyzed over the entire span of the twentieth century, the decades would blend together into an overall description of a *century of change* — automobiles, airplanes, radio, television, atomic bomb, synthetic materials, Hubble space craft, computers, cellular telephones, World Wide Web, etc.

Historians look at the past in a similar manner. They have identified large periods of time in Western civilization during which its members took a similar mental approach to all aspects of living, whether it be social customs, politics, religion, art, architecture, literature, theater, or music. Of course, these time periods overlap, sometimes by hundreds of years. Never will a society wake up one morning and decide to change its way of thinking, but little by little, the trends of one period give way to trends of another period, then to another, etc. The periods generally agreed to are as follows:

MEDIEVAL	450A.D.	–	1400
RENAISSANCE	1400	–	1600
BAROQUE	1600	–	1750
CLASSICAL	1750	–	1825
ROMANTIC	1825	–	1900
CONTEMPORARY	1900	–	Present

The change from any one period to another is sometimes described as a change from a *classical* approach to life to a *romantic* approach, or vice versa. (The style periods called Classical and Romantic got these names because at the time the names were adopted, only the eighteenth and nineteenth centuries were given much analytical attention.) The word

classical

romantic

classical means following a prescribed model for achieving success, objectivity, fixed routines, clarity of formal design, balance, formulas, status quo, simplicity, and craftsmanship. The term **romantic** means breaking away from set models, subjectivity, imagination, sensuality, exploration, and challenging the status quo. It has been recognized that each historic period, though the emphasis may change as the period moves on and though there is always an overlapping of the two tendencies, will have a dominant tendency toward either a classical or a romantic outlook at any given time. Keep these concepts in mind as the style periods are briefly outlined below. The music terms will be explained in future chapters.

The music of the early Middle Ages was a continuation of what had been established in earlier times by the cultures around the Mediterranean. The music is thought to have had the characteristics still heard in traditional music of eastern cultures — monophonic, flowing, asymmetrical, of conjunct movement, ornamented. As a separate Western civilization began to develop, the Christian church was a strong unifying force, partially through its insistence that conformity be maintained, including conformity in music. The only music to be performed during church worship services was the officially sanctioned Gregorian chants. During the ninth century, church musicians began to experiment with the chants. This started as a simple pitch-per-pitch harmonization, but by the twelfth century, elaborate three and four part polyphony was flourishing. This spirit of musical exploration was expanded during the Renaissance period, but by the end of the period the counter-reformation within the Catholic church, along with a spirit of absolute rule in monarchies in non-Catholic areas, led to a more classical frame of mind and musical compositions of greater simplicity and conventionalism. The Baroque period brought with it an influx of new ideas. Opera not only introduced a form of theater that was appealing to all social classes, but the demands necessary to present the dialogue of individual characters through music required that the elaborate polyphony of the Renaissance give way to homophony. Polyphony continued to flourish, however, in the new attention given to instrumental music. But, by the end of the Baroque period, the music was becoming more and more stylized. Phrases and music sections of symmetrical proportions and predictable harmonic patterns introduced the Classical period. The emphasis of the period was on homophony and the clarity of music statements. The role of each instrument of the orchestra was well defined. The Romantic spirit brought on expansion and re-evaluation of all previous musical notions. The invention of fingering keys and valves allowed for new instrumental ideas and more complex technical demands. The size of the orchestra grew. Melodies became long and intertwined, and moods within a single movement of a composition could change abruptly. Also, changing abruptly were the conventional rules of harmony. Basic chords were extended to a point of having a vague and nebulous key center. The twentieth century continues the romantic spirit. In fact, many historians will state that the Romantic style period is continuing to the present day.

Listening Composition

NOCTURNE IN E MINOR
Romantic Style Period

FREDERIC CHOPIN
1810-1849

Frederic Chopin was born near Warsaw, Poland to a French father and a Polish mother. His father taught French to the children of the Polish nobility. As a young child, Chopin studied piano at the Warsaw School of Music. He gave his first public recital when he was only eight years old, was a published composer at the age of 15, and was widely known for both performance and composition by the time he was 19.

When Chopin was 21, he traveled to Paris to give concerts, and decided to settle there permanently. The French aristocracy immediately accepted him, and he became part of a circle of well-known artists, musicians and writers, such as Victor Hugo, Alexandre Dumas, Robert Schumann, Eugene Delacroix, and Franz Liszt. It was Liszt who would later introduce him to the female writer

George Sand (Amadine Aurore Lucie Dupin), with whom he would have a very intense ten-year relationship.

Frederic Chopin's early renown was established as a brilliant concert pianist. He was famous for his subtle and refined playing. He composed almost exclusively for the piano, having an intimate knowledge of the full range of capabilities of that instrument. His compositions have a truly distinctive style.

Chopin has been called "the poet of the piano." A fellow pianist and composer, a Russian named Anton Rubinstein, said this about Chopin:

> *The piano bard, the piano rhapsodist, the piano mind, the piano soul is Chopin. Tragic, romantic, lyric, heroic, dramatic, fantastic, soulful, sweet, dreamy, brilliant, grand, simple. All possible expressions are found in his compositions, and all are sung by him upon his instrument.*

A shy, reserved man, Chopin preferred the atmosphere of aristocratic salons to that of concert halls. He lived in luxury, partly because he taught piano to the children of the very rich. Although he was considered an excellent teacher, it is difficult to say if his students knew that he lamented, "They watch their hands while playing, and play wrong notes with great feeling. Eccentric people, God help them."

Like many people who lived during this time, Frederic Chopin suffered from the effects of tuberculosis for many years. He was frail, and often physically exhausted. Beginning with a respiratory ailment in 1838–39 on the island of Majorca, Chopin's illness was not properly diagnosed until 1847. In 1848, Chopin's dwindling health was severe during a concert tour of England and Scotland. In a letter to a friend, Chopin wrote:

> *As regards my future, matters are going from bad to worse. I grow weaker and weaker, and cannot compose anything at all. All morning, and until two o'clock, I am good for nothing. Later, when I am dressed, everything oppresses me and I gasp until dinner. At bedtime I am at liberty to gasp and dream until the same thing begins again.*

That same year Frederic Chopin returned to Paris. He died in 1849.

Representative Composition

NOCTURNE IN E MINOR

Type of Composition: **Piano Solo**

Overview: The word "nocturne" is a French term that literally means "of the night." Thus, one thinks of music for reflection and relaxation during the evening after dinner. Typically, nocturnes are short piano pieces, usually homophonic with the main melodies heard from the right hand while the left hand supplies an "arpeggio" (the notes of a chord played separately in some sequential order) accompaniment.

Structure: **Simple Song Form (Expanded).** This composition is made of six phrases. Moreover, phrases 1, 2, 4, and 5 are parallel. Phrases 3 and 6 are parallel. Simple song form is usually "simple"—two long parallel phrases. In this Chopin nocturne, however, —true to the spirit of the romantic period—the form is greatly expanded, using elements common to binary form, sonata form, and theme and variation form. With detail left to the "commentary" below, the overall structure could be summarized as follows: The composition consists of two parallel "phrase groups," each constructed of three phrases, two parallel and one contrasting (aab). Thus, the structure is: Introduction, Phrase Group 1 (aab), and Phrase Group II (aab).

TIME	PHRASE GROUP	PHRASE	COMMENTARY
0:00	**Introduction**		The song begins with a simple left-hand arpeggio.

0:05	I	a	The main melody of the composition is introduced by the right hand of the pianist. The arpeggio pattern by the left hand, which was begun in the introduction, continues, serving as an accompaniment. Thus, a homophonic texture is created. The overall direction of the melody, though rising slightly in the middle, is downward.
0:41		a	This phrase is parallel to the first. However, shortly after the main melody is begun, the direction changes briefly, using the octave to create a small climax. Then, also by means of the octave, the direction continues to be downward. The phrase, as did the first, rises to a middle range, but unlike the first, does not descend. It stays within the same pitch range, elongating the phrase by means of many harmonic changes, taking the listener through the keys of C Major and D Minor before coming to rest in the new key of B Major.
1:40		b	This phrase serves as coda to the musical material presented in phrases 1 and 2. It uses new melodic material, the overall direction being downward. The phrase is very unique in its musical purpose. It is too short to be considered apart from the first two phrases, but bears little resemblance to them.However, without this concluding thought, the composition would lack an extremely dynamic and moving element. Harmonic tension is added to the end of this phrase (in the key of B Major), which draws the listener back to the key of E Minor.
2:16	II	a	The return to the main melody is true to its first hearing in terms of 1) identical length and 2) an almost note-for-note accompaniment (only six notes different).

		However, the melody is elaborately ornamented to the point where it could be called a free variation instead of a repetition. The notes are in the high pitch range, and the dynamic level is primarily forte, even though the level of piano is briefly used before a crescendo elevates the volume to is previous position.
2:52	a	The melody is heard in octaves and at a forte dynamic level. The octaves continue as a crescendo to a fortissimo level and the use of repeated notes provide the final climax of the composition. The tension is then relaxed as a decrescendo takes the dynamic level to piano. The phrase, having begun in the key of E Minor, closes in E Major.
3:27	b	This phrase again serves as a coda, this time to the entire composition, starting and ending in the key of E Major and reflecting the downward movement of the entire song.

Chapter 9

MUSIC CHARACTERISTICS OF THE STYLE PERIODS

MEDIEVAL

Rhythm: Gregorian chant employed unmeasured rhythm; later organum used rhythmic modes emphasizing triple meter; secular music used a steady, metered pulse when used for dancing.

Melody: Mostly conjunct, limited pitch range; shape of songs with words tended to follow speech inflections.

Harmony: No harmony in early Middle Ages; organum stressed the open sounds of unisons, fourths, fifths, and octaves.

Texture: Monophonic in early Middle Ages; later Middle Ages introduced polyphonic texture built on a Gregorian chant cantus firmus; two three, sometimes four voices.

Expression: Followed speech inflections when words were sung.

Form: Gregorian chant, organum, Mass, motet; dance forms, including the estampie and carole.

RENAISSANCE

Rhythm: Measured rhythms; duple meter becomes more common in sacred music.

Melody: Mostly conjunct; pitch range is wider than in Middle Ages.

Harmony: Open sounds still stressed, but the closed consonant intervals of thirds and sixths become acceptable; cadences pull toward a keytone, but the strong establishment of a tonal center is not fully developed.

Texture: Complex polyphony using cantus firmus technique; the official chant could be paraphrased or another melody used; cantus firmus could appear in any voice part; use of imitation, canonic technique, word painting, enigmas; compositions written for four, five, six, eight, up to forty independent voice parts.

Expression: Voices combined with instruments; consorts of instruments, harpsichord, improvements in organ construction.

Form: Mass, motet (sacred and secular), madrigal, chorale, anthem; ricercare, fantasia, diferencia, toccata; dance forms, including the pavane and galliard.

BAROQUE

Rhythm:	Continuous running rhythm, usually in the bass line; pulse did not normally change until a slight ritardando at the end of the composition.
Melody:	Much use of imitation and sequences; melodies were often ornamented; firm establishment of major and minor scales.
Harmony:	Use of functional harmony directed toward a strong tonal center.
Texture:	Polyphonic and homophonic with both supported by basso continuo (running bass part plus chords).
Expression:	Terraced dynamics; no use of crescendo and decrescendo.
Form:	Opera, oratorio, cantata; trio sonata; dance suite, concerto, concerto grosso, fugue, chorale prelude; binary form dominates.

CLASSICAL

Rhythm:	Steady pulse, clearly defined meter, some use of rubato in slower pieces; ritardando may occur at all major cadence points.
Melody:	Elegant, tuneful melodies of symmetrical phrases; use of light trills and melodic turns, running scale patterns extending over a wide pitch range.
Harmony:	Very strong tonal center; generally predictable harmonic progressions.
Texture:	Primarily homophonic, but polyphony was common in longer compositions; textures could change frequently.
Expression:	Wide dynamic range, crescendos and decrescendos were common; piano replaces harpsichord as principal keyboard instrument; fingering keys and valves placed on wind instruments.
Form:	Opera, Mass, sonata, rondo; string quartet, symphony, concerto; ternary form, sonata-allegro form, theme and variations.

ROMANTIC

Rhythm: Tempo could change abruptly, rubato was freely used, some use of indefinite and asymmetrical meters, rhythm is quite complicated at times.

Melody: Flowing melodies, technically difficult skips and runs in instrumental music, phrases are asymmetrical at times, use of a wide pitch range, use of leitmotifs.

Harmony: Still rooted in chords built on triads, but the use of extended chords to the point where the tonal center becomes vague at times; many key center changes within one composition; harmony is complex.

Texture: Primarily homophonic but often with elaborate accompaniments; elaborate polyphony used in instrumental music, but generally with a predominant flowing theme.

Expression: Large orchestra, music is very emotional and subjective, dynamic range uses the extremes of soft and loud, many mood changes.

Form: Continuation of classical forms, many works for solo piano, art song, song cycle, symphonic tone poem.

CONTEMPORARY

Rhythm: Complex rhythms, many meter changes, asymmetrical, indefinite, different meters simultaneously.

Melody: Short, disjunct, atonal melodic fragments; many skips, wide ranges demanded for both instruments and voice; scales of other cultures are utilized.

Harmony: Atonal or incorporates several tonal centers simultaneously; great use of dissonant intervals of seconds and sevenths, clashes of sounds; chords built on intervals other than thirds; twelve-tone compositional technique.

Texture: Extremes of texture from very thin to very dense; much use of polyphony, but with short abrupt melodic statements instead of clearly defined motives and melodies.

Expression: New technical demands of instruments, sprechstimme, extreme weight given to individual interpretation and subjectivity.

Form: Free form, chance music, forms based on mathematical permutations, musique concrete, computers, synthesizers.

Listening Composition

SYMPHONY NO. 4, 4ᵗʰ mvt.
Romantic Style Period

JOHANNES BRAHMS
1833-1897

Born in Hamburg, Germany, Johannes Brahms was the son of a bass player for the Hamburg opera. He first studied music with his father. By the time he was 13, he was spending his days studying piano, music theory and composition, and spending his nights making a living by playing piano in taverns and bordellos. A talented pianist, Brahms gave his first public recital at age 14.

At the age of 20, Johannes Brahms went on his first concert tour as an accompanist for the Hungarian violinist Eduard Remenyi. During this tour, Brahms met Franz Liszt, and Robert and Clara Schumann. Liszt had much praise for the young Brahms, but the two never became friendly. It was the Schumanns who would ultimately shape Brahms' life and musical career.

Robert Schumann hailed the young composer as "the coming genius of German music," and published a magazine article in which he called Brahms "a musical messiah." Schumann also arranged to have Brahms' first works published.

While Brahms was preparing new works for his publisher, Robert Schumann had a nervous collapse and was committed to an asylum. Clara was left with seven children to support. Brahms came to live in the Schumann home to help care for the children, and stayed there for two years.

Though living in the Romantic period, Johannes Brahms is sometimes thought of as a "misplaced classicist." While his contemporaries were discussing the music of the future, Brahms sought to emulate models from the past. He admired Bach, Haydn, Mozart, and especially Beethoven. His musical style is his own, but it has its roots in the works of these composers. He had a vast knowledge of the music that came before him; he collected music manuscripts and edited baroque and classical compositions. He was drawn to classical forms, but interpreted these using the resources of his own time. Brahms was fully aware that some considered his style "unfashionable," remarking that he had been born too late.

When Brahms was passed over for the position of conductor of the Philharmonic Orchestra in Hamburg, a position he desperately wanted, he moved to Vienna. He worked as a choral conductor for almost four years, and then conducted the orchestra of the Society of the Friends of Music from 1872 to 1875. His experience as a conductor influenced him dramatically. He devoted himself almost entirely to composition after 1875.

Brahms created many masterpieces: four symphonies, four concertos, over 200 songs, many piano pieces, choral music, and numerous chamber pieces. The only traditional musical form in which he did not write was opera.

In outward appearance, it is said that Brahms often was quite rude. At one gathering, he rose to leave, stopped at the door, turned and said, "If there is anyone here whom I have not insulted, I beg your pardon." Inwardly, however, he was shy and agreeable. He was very supportive of and helpful to talented young musicians, perhaps because of the help he himself was given as a youngster by Robert Schumann.

Brahms' sensitivity and faith are demonstrated in his *Four Serious Songs*, set to biblical texts, dedicated to his friend Clara Schumann as she lay dying in 1896. Brahms died a year later.

Representative Composition

SYMPHONY NO. 4, 4th Mvt.

Type of Composition: **Movement from a symphony**

Overview: Brahms composed this symphony during the summers of 1884 and 1885 in the city of Meiningen. Before its first performance in that city, Brahms was concerned that the work would not be well received by the people of this small town located in the Styrian Alps of Austria. Such was not the case. However, there were hisses in the audience at its first performance in the more sophisticated Vienna. Little by little the Viennese turned their praise to this work, however, and at a performance one month before Brahms' death, it is said that applause was spontaneous after each movement.

Structure: **Combination of Ternary Form and Theme and Variations.** The composition is unified in two ways. First, the strong ABA structure of ternary form presents a large section of music, followed by a contrasting section, then a return to the theme and mood of the first section. The sections themselves, however, reveal the second unifying force: The entire composition is a set of continuous variations based on the opening theme. The technique of *continuous* variations was developed during the Baroque period. Brahms' love for that period is shown not only in this choice of form (a singular example of Romantic period symphonic compositions), but also in the fact that the theme itself is based on a melody found in J.S. Bach's Cantata No. 150: *Unto Thee, O Lord, I Lift Up My Soul.* Combining the two forms, the result is Section A = Theme + Variations 1–11. Section B = Variations 12–15. Section A' = Variations 16–30. A final Coda (Variations 31–34) brings the movement to a close.

TIME	SECTION	VARIATION	COMMENTARY
0:00	A		The theme, marked to be played energetically and passionately, is introduced by the brass and wood-wind instruments.
0:16		1–11	These eleven variations are built on the theme melody and, especially, the underlying harmony. Many changes of mood, instrumentation, and dynamics occur.
3:12	B	12–15	The tempo is much slower (the beat is twice the length of the beat of the opening section). A legato flute solo with string accompaniment introduces this section. Clarinet, oboe, and flute then exchange dialogue, followed by slow-moving brass chords. The very end of this section returns to a flute solo playing a descending passage, concluding with a ritardando and a fermata.
6:00	A	16–30	The opening theme returns, followed by variations which utilize mood changes, crescendos, decrescendos, and sudden dynamic shifts. Strings and woodwinds dominate this section.
9:25	Coda	31–34	Brass instruments and woodwinds restate the theme over fast-moving strings as the tempo becomes faster. An ascending melody played by the trombones helps the music continue to build. The music continues to accelerate until the final chord.

Chapter 10
SEPARATION OF EAST AND WEST

When a person of the Western world hears traditional music of China, India, or the Middle East, the sound is strange and unfamiliar. The melodies are long, ornamented, and conjunct. They lack distinctive phrasing and symmetry, and are presented without harmony or harmonic accompaniment. These used to be the characteristics of the music of Western Europe.

The Greek civilization which included the Italian Peninsula, the Middle East, and Northern Africa, was of Eastern culture. When the Romans conquered the Greeks, they did very little to change the culture. The Romans were of a practical mind, giving attention to warfare, government, legal procedures, and engineering, but leaving philosophy, mind, and the arts as the Greeks had developed them.

By 450 AD the Roman Empire had disintegrated due to internal corruption and attacks by barbarians. The empire began to divide itself into separate and independent geographical regions. The Latin language began to change within those regions to present-day Italian, Spanish, Portuguese, French, and Romanian. Within these areas, the feudal system developed. A "lord," living in relative luxury (brought about by taxation), maintained a standing army in order to protect and oversee many destitute and illiterate peasants.

LITURGICAL MUSIC

Gregorian chant

During this time, the only stabilizing force was the Christian church — the Roman Catholic church. This institution maintained the Latin language and unified social customs and artistic expression. The music sung during worship, derived from its ancient roots, was very oriental in nature. The songs of the Christian church, compiled and cataloged by Pope Gregory (540-609 AD) at the beginning of the seventh century, became known as **Gregorian chant.** More than 3000 Gregorian chants still survive.

Gregorian Chant

A Gregorian chant typically is monophonic, nonmetrical, of a limited pitch range, conjunct motion, and the words are in Latin. The rhythm follows the free flow of speech, and the melodic contour rises and falls according to the text. To express the words, a chant might be syllabic, neumatic, or melismatic:

syllabic

Syllabic — one pitch per syllable of text:

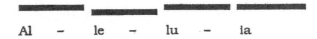

Al – le – lu – ia

neumatic

Neumatic — Two or three pitches per text:

Al – le – lu – ia

melismatic

Melismatic — Many pitches per syllable:

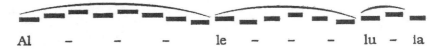

Al – – – le – – – lu – ia

Early Polyphony

The monasteries and schools of the Christian church were active educational institutions and social centers. All manner of topics were discussed — religion, philosophy, mathematics, science — and concerns met — hospitals, orphanages, care of the elderly, importance of the individual. This critical and analytical attitude carried over into all aspects of life, including music. During the ninth century, experiments in adding harmonizing pitches to the Gregorian chant melodies were begun. At first, these added pitches were placed at a fixed distance of either four pitches or five pitches above each original chant pitch. This early harmony was called **organum**, and the method of harmonization just described is called **parallel organum**. The official melody, called the **vox principales** or **cantus firmus**, had to be strictly maintained when the new part, the **vox organalis** or **duplum**, was added. The added part eventually became most elaborate. Instead of one new pitch with a given pitch of the chant, two or three pitches might be used, then four or five or many. The added part became extremely melismatic and completely independent of the chant. This truly polyphonic music is known as **melismatic organum**. As before, the official chant had to be maintained, but as the vox organalis became more and more elaborate, the pitches of the vox principales were lengthened in order to accomodate it. Eventually, the pitches of the chant melody were "stretched out" to a point where the chant itself, although present and serving as a foundation, was no longer recognizable.

organum
parallel organum
vox principales
cantus firmus
vox organalis
duplum

melismatic
organum

In liturgical services at which both men and women were present, only men were allowed to sing. Then, as the pitch range was expanded, the high parts were sung by boys. Women participated in music making in the secular world and in worship services attended only by women.

131

The height of melismatic organum occurred in the twelfth century at the Cathedral of Notre Dame. Two composers, Leonin and Perotin (only their first names are known), combined three and even four independent melodies. Thus, just as a new *Western* way of viewing the world — a way based on analysis of a problem, skeptical attitude, individuality and stimulation of the senses — had emerged, so a new type of music, based on harmony and independent melody lines, was leading farther and farther away from its Eastern roots.

SECULAR MUSIC

Secular music of the Middle Ages was performed for festivals, dances, celebrations, etc. — just as is popular music of our time. Also, music was a means to tell a story or simply entertain an audience.

Secular music is more difficult to trace than Liturgical music because it was seldom written down, and because a well-known song might continue to be popular over a long time period. However, some information is known about two groups of musicians and entertainers.

Troubadours, Trouveres, Minnesingers

troubadours
trouveres
minnesingers

The **troubadours** of southern France in the twelfth and thirteenth centuries had counterparts in northern France, the **trouveres**, and in Germany, the **minnesingers**. Although the style of poetry and music was imitated by other social classes, the troubadours, trouveres, and minnesingers were primarily of the noble class. They wrote poems of courtly love, the beauty or hostility of nature, and knightly heroic deeds.

songs of geste

These poems collectively known as **songs of geste** were often set to music and sung either by the poet or by an accompanying musician-servant. One of the most popular of these songs during that time period told the story of Robin Hood and Maid Marion.

Jongleurs and Minstrels

jongleurs
minstrels

The **jongleurs** and **minstrels** of the Middle Ages were poor itinerant entertainers. Moving from village to village, they would attempt to amuse, hopefully for a meager donation, any audience willing to give them attention. They did this by means of acrobatics, trained animals, story telling, magic tricks, music, and dance.

A jongleur or minstrel was fortunate indeed if he were accepted for a permanent position in a court or as a servant to a wandering troubadour. In the later Middle Ages — the thirteenth century — the status of the jongleurs and minstrels was somewhat elevated, even to the point of some towns offering paid positions to town musicians responsible for civic festivals and ceremonies.

Aerophones of the Middle Ages and Renaissance

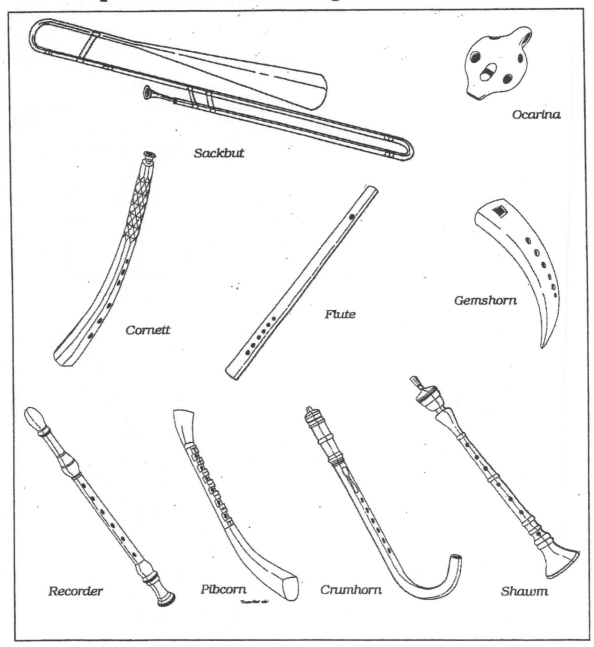

Sackbut

Ocarina

Cornett

Flute

Gemshorn

Recorder

Pibcorn

Crumhorn

Shawm

Chordophones of the Middle Ages and Renaissance

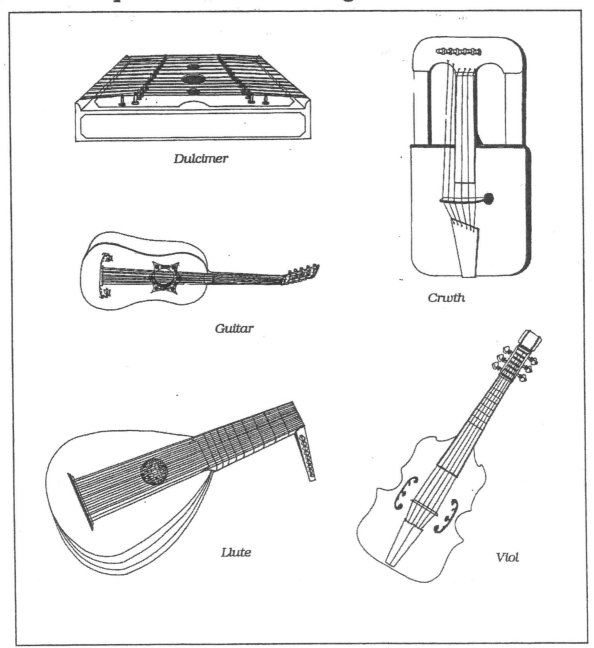

Dulcimer

Crwth

Guitar

Llute

Viol

Listening Composition

PRELUDE TO THE AFTERNOON OF A FAUN
Romantic Style Period

CLAUDE DEBUSSY
1862-1918

Claude Debussy was born in Saint-Germain-en-Laye, near Paris, France. He had his first piano lesson at the age of nine, and in 1873 he began his studies at the Paris Conservatory. His teachers there considered him a talented rebel.

In the early 1880's, Debussy met Nadezhda von Meck, a wealthy woman who offered a yearly allowance to Peter Ilyitch Tchaikovsky, whom she greatly admired, so that he could devote himself to his music. Through her, Tchaikovsky hired Debussy as a pianist for the summers. Debussy traveled with the von Meck family to Italy, Switzerland and Russia. The Russian school of music was a great influence on Debussy's early style.

Winning the prestigious Prix de Rome in 1884, Debussy was able to study in Rome. But his musical inspiration waned there, and he left after the required two years of study.

From 1887 on, Debussy rarely appeared in public as a performer. He devoted his time to composition. He was more comfortable in cafes, preferring the company of writers, artists and *night people* to that of musicians. He became close friends with several of the Symbolist poets. In fact, many of Debussy's songs are based on Paul Verlaine's poems, and Stephane Mallarme's poem inspired his first, and most famous, orchestral work, Prelude to the Afternoon of a Faun.

Debussy was influenced by many different styles of music. While visiting the Paris Exposition in 1889, he heard the exotic sounds performed by a Javanese gamelan (an Indonesian orchestra composed mainly of percussion instruments). He had also traveled to Germany to hear the opera productions of Richard Wagner's works. Debussy, who had already rejected traditional musical theory and form, admired Wagner's music but was also repelled by its philosophical implications. A clue to his feelings can be gotten from the way he signed his name: "Claude Debussy, French musician."

Debussy rejected the established rules. Instead, he wanted to create a certain atmosphere or mood through his music. Although his works set the standards by which impressionistic music is measured, Debussy despised the term *impressionism*. He believed that it was merely a French reaction to German romanticism. He reacted to his experiences, rather than *reality*. He believed music should be entertaining and pleasant. He delighted in sound for the sake of sound, and used conventional instruments and methods in unconventional ways. Regarding music, he stated, "There is no theory. You have only to listen. Pleasure is the law."

His personal life seemed to be in turmoil. He married a dressmaker named Rosalie Texier in 1899. When he left her in 1904 for Emma Bardac, the wife of a Parisian banker, Rosalie attempted suicide. He married Bardac in 1908, and they had a daughter, Claude-Emma. He was always borrowing money. He hated appearing in public but went on concert tours of Europe to maintain his high standard of living.

Around 1910, Debussy developed cancer. The toll this took on his strength is evident in his inability to produce any large works during his final years. Although many pieces were planned, few were completed. The sadness he felt at the onset of World War I contributed to the deterioration of his health. He died in Paris in 1918 as German shells bombed his beloved city.

Representative Composition

PRELUDE TO THE AFTERNOON OF A FAUN

Type of Composition: **Tone Poem.** The tone poem (also known as a "symphonic poem") was developed in the Romantic period. It is a one-movement orchestral work which gives a musical interpretation of a picture, literary work, scene from nature, philosophical idea, or other non-musical inspiration. Such is the case with Claude Debussy's composition illustrating the poem "Afternoon of a Faun" by Stephane Mallarme. The story is of a faun, the mythological half-man, half-goat, who dreams of love with two beautiful nymphs in a primordial forest.

Structure: **Ternary Form (A–B–A).** This form, loosely constructed by Debussy, corresponds to the story as the faun wakes from slumber (A), encounters the nymphs (B), then returns to sleep (A).

TIME	SECTION	COMMENTARY
0:00	A	The flute, without accompaniment, opens the composition with the expressive, "dreamy" main theme. When other instruments enter, the texture remains primarily thin. The harp adds to the fanciful imagery. Much imitation and repetition is used. The main theme is heard a total of five times in this section, but each presentation is varied and embellished.
2:45	Interlude	The mood changes as the clarinet hauntingly enters. A very nebulous structure maintains the vagueness of dreaming while the music slowly proceeds to the next section.
4:32	B	A new theme is presented by the woodwinds, embellished at length, then played by the strings. Momentum begins to pick up as the music leads to the only "fortissimo" in the composition. A duet between clarinet and violin at a pianissimo dynamic level brings this section to a close.
6:20	A	The main theme returns, continuing to be fragmented and embellished. The flute, harp, oboe, English horn, cello, violin, and small bells (called antique cymbals) are the main instruments. The composition ends quietly.

Chapter 11
THE DEVELOPMENT OF COMPOSITIONAL TECHNIQUES

As the spirit of intellectualism from the late Middle Ages continued into the Renaissance, more thought was given to logic, organization and a more comprehensive view of music. It is no coincidence that the Renaissance enthusiasm over keeping accurate financial accounts, inventory of merchandise, scientific analysis, and confidence in human potential to accomplish a task is reflected in music composition.

COMPOSITIONAL TECHNIQUES

Repetition and Imitation

repetition
imitation

Rudimentary techniques of organization are **repetition**, the restating of a position of music, and **imitation**, a musical statement that identifiably resembles a previously heard statement. These devices are unifying elements, giving a composition a sense of wholeness instead of a compilation of unrelated parts.

A polyphonic composition based on strict imitation is created when a single melody is constructed in such a way that it can continuously intertwine with itself. This strict imitation is

canon

round

caccia
chasse

canonic technique

quodlibet

called a **canon**, a composition in which a melody in one part is followed at a short distance by the same melody in another part, so that the melody overlaps itself. In America, we recognize this type of composition as a **round**. The intellectual process needed to compose a canon was intriguing to the Renaissance mind. The earliest written example of a canon still in existence comes from Italy where that type of composition was known as a **caccia**, meaning a "hunt" or "chase." This is very similar to the parallel French word **chasse**.

Most composers will not write complete works that are solely canons. In canons, the element of unity is very strong, but variety is lacking. Therefore, a composition may utilize areas where the initial impression is imitation, as if a canon were beginning, but then strict imitation is abandoned in favor of freely composed polyphony. In this case the composer is using **canonic technique**, but the result is not a pure canon. This imitative practice can be seen in compositions with such generic names as toccata, fantasia, capriccio, canzona, ricercare, and fugue.

If the writing of a canon can be considered an intellectual puzzle, another puzzle is the **quodlibet** — two or more well-known songs that have been found to sound good when performed at the same time. Below are the words to two American folk songs that sound good when sung together.

WHEN THE SAINTS GO MARCHING IN

Oh, when the saints go marching in,
Oh, when the saints go marching in,
Lord, I want to be in that number,
When the saints go marching in.

RED RIVER VALLEY

Come and sit by my side if you love me,
Do not hasten to bid me adieu,
But remember the Red River Valley,
And the one who has loved you so true.

The Renaissance composer enjoyed the mental exercise involved in canonic music and quodlibets, hiding a well-known song in an inner part of a serious composition, using a well-known song written backwards as a cantus firmus, and other musical puzzles. The general name for musical mysteries is **enigmatic music**.

enigmatic music

Word Painting

When music is added to words, often the composer also wants to express the sentiment of text. Often this can be accomplished in very specific ways. For example, if the words *run* or *hurry* were encountered, a composer might utilize fast notes or a quick rhythm. If words referred to birds or mountains, high pitches might give the impression of *looking up* or *in the sky*. In the Renaissance, a practice of dedicating a musical composition to a person who died was to end the composition with an ascending scale passage, as if to describe the person's ascension to heaven — although one such composition for a person who was not well-like ended with a downward moving scale passage. The use of musical elements to describe or paint a picture of the text of a song is called **word painting**. Add the indicated expression as you read an advertisement to bring tourists to Mount Lemon near Tucson, Arizona.

word painting

Take a quick trip along the w^{i}n$_d$i^{n}g road to the high country

and the 9,000 foot e^l^{e}^{v}^{a}^{t}^{i}^{o}^{n} of Mount Lemon. You may never want to c$_o$$_m$$_e$ $_d$$_o$$_w$n.

madrigal
madrigale
chanson
lied

Word painting was widely used in the Renaissance, again reflecting that period's interest in a combination of musical expression and intellectual foundation. It is often heard in a popular type of composition known as a **madrigal**, a short lyric poem set to music, usually polyphonic for three to eight voices. Madrigals, known in other countries as the **madrigale** (Italy), **chanson** (France) and **lied** (Germany) demanded a high level of musical training in order to be sung. The middle and upper classes of the Renaissance had that training. In fact, it was commonly expected that a person would be able to read music and sing well enough to carry one of the parts of a madrigal. One of the most prolific composers of madrigals, Thomas Morley, began his music studies late. Being humiliated by his inabilities, he eventually learned to read and write music and became highly acclaimed during his time. But, in the introduction to his first book of madrigals he wrote:

> *This book rose out of an occasion when I had been embarrassed while at the home of an acquaintance. Supper being ended and, according to the custom, the music books handed out, the hostess invited me to sing. But, after many excuses, I protested unfeignedly that I could not sing, everyone began to wonder, ye, some began to whisper how I was brought up.*

MUSICAL FORM

As a house or building — or a human body — must have a solid underlying structure in order to stand alone, so must a music composition, at least from the standpoint of the Western mind. In Greek, Roman and other Eastern cultures, time was not important. Even today, Mediterranean societies and societies of Latin descent are said to live in the *eternal present* — times set for appointments are *approximate*; if you need to take a little longer in order to do a better job, take the time; if you want to close the shop and go fishing, go fishing. But with the emergence of Western thought, *things must get accomplished, time is of the essence, a formula can solve any problem, set up an assembly line,* etc. This approach to life may have developed from the Christian view that the human is put on earth for a purpose. There is only one lifetime to accomplish this purpose. There is no second chance. This is contrary to the Eastern concept of reincarnation where existence is viewed as falling and rising spirals, and eternity is unpredictable. In Eastern music this is reflected in melodies, including Gregorian chants, that are free to wander without direction or structure. But, in the West, music must have audible definition, goal, and completion. The element of definition comes by means of an overall design and an underlying foundational structure. Design and structure constitute what is known as **form**. The form of a given composition generally can be placed in one of two categories, continuous form or sectional form.

form

Continuous Form

Compositions which cannot be broken into separate independent bodies are said to be in **continuous form** or **through composed form**. This means that music begins and continues with only new material until the end. A nonmusic example of continuous form is a key:

**continuous form
through composed
form**

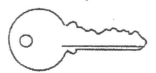

The unifying devices of motives and imitation may be used, but material is never repeated in the same way as previously heard. Also, the unifying techniques of **augmentation**, making the durations of the pitches of a motive or melody longer;

augmentation

diminution
inversion
retrograde

diminution, making the duration of the pitches shorter; **inversion**, presenting a motive or melody upside down; and **retrograde**, writing a motive or melody backwards, may be employed.

Sectional Form

sectional form
simple song form

A musical composition that can be broken down into larger well-defined units of material are said to be in **sectional form**. The starting point in the study of sectional form is the organization called **simple song form**. This form consists of only one section and could almost be considered through composed if it weren't for the fact that the music usually consists of two parallel phrases. The first verse of MARY HAD A LITTLE LAMB is a simple song form.

> Mary had a little lamb,
> Little lamb, little lamb,
> Mary had a little lamb,
> Its fleece was white as snow.

strophic

If additional verses of MARY HAD A LITTLE LAMB are performed, the form is said to be **strophic** — the repetition of a song over and over again. If the melody of MARY HAD A LITTLE LAMB were identified by the letter **A**, three verses would appear as **A A A**.

>   Mary had a little lamb,
> **A** Little lamb, little lamb,
>   Mary had a little lamb,
>   Its fleece was white as snow.
>
>   Followed her to school one day,
> **A** School one day, school one day,
>   Followed her to school one day,
>   Which was against the rule.
>
>   Made the children laugh and play,
> **A** Laugh and play, laugh and play,
>   Made the children laugh and play,
>   To see a lamb at school.

additive

Sectional Forms may also be **additive**, meaning that new music sections are added to existing sections. Consider the familiar I'VE BEEN WORKING ON THE RAILROAD:

        I've been working on the railroad all the live long day,

A   I've been working on the railroad just to pass the time away.

        Can't you hear the whistle blowing, rise up so early in the morn,

        Can't you hear the captain shouting, "Dinah, blow your horn."

        Dinah, won't you blow, Dinah, won't you blow,

B   Dinah, won't you blow your horn?

        Dinah, won't you blow, Dinah, won't you blow,

        Dinah, won't you blow your horn?

        Someone's in the kitchen with Dinah,

C   Someone's in the kitchen I know,

        Someone's in the kitchen with Dinah,

        Strumming on the old banjo.

        Fee, fi, fiddley - ah - ee,

D   Fee, fi, fiddley - ah - oh,

        Fee, fi, fiddley - ah - ee,

        Strumming on the old banjo.

The addition of sections results in the form **A B C D**.

trinary form

binary form

Compositions in additive form could, of course, be of any length, i.e., **A B C D E F G**, etc. And, while the **trinary form** of **A B C** was fairly common in the Renaissance, over the centuries the most widely used additive form has been simply **A B**, called **binary form**. YANKEE DOODLE is an example of binary form.

        Yankee Doodle went to town,

A   Riding on a pony,

        Stuck a feather in his hat,

        And called it macaroni.

Yankee Doodle keep it up,
B Yankee Doodle dandy,
Mind the music and the step,
And with the girls be handy.

A common practice developed during the Baroque period was to repeat each of the sections for unifying purposes. The result can be diagramed **A A B B**. The human body could be analyzed as having this form:

theme with variations

Another additive form is **theme with variations**, a composition in which a song is repeated over and over but with changes to either melody, harmony, or rhythm with each repetition. The general requirement, again for the purpose of unifying the comprehension of the composition, is that enough of the original song is presented in each repetition to allow the listener to follow the music clearly. Theme with variations form is often outlined $A\ A^1\ A^2\ A^3$, etc. Jazz players make extensive use of it as they play a melody, then allow individual soloists to take turns improvising variations based on that melody.

return forms

ternary form

Sectional forms called **return forms** bring circular unity and final completion to the overall musical construction by repeating previously heard sections. The most common of these is the **ternary form**, consisting of a section of music, a contrasting section, and a return to the first section – **A B A**. This concept is the most common used in the structure of popular music, even *old* popular music like the song FIVE FOOT TWO.

A
> Five foot two,
> Eyes of blue,
> But, oh what those five feet could do,
> Has anybody seen my gal?

A
> Turned up nose,
> Turned down hose,
> A flapper, yes sir, one of those,
> Has anybody seen my gal?

B
> Now if you run into a five foot two,
> covered with fur,
> Diamond rings, all those things,
> You can bet your life it isn't her,

A
> But, could she love,
> Could she woo,
> Could she, could she, could she coo,
> Has anybody seen my gal?

rondo

Another example of a return form is the **rondo** where one or more sections are returned to at intervals.

Examples are: **A B A C A**

A B A C A D A

A B A C A B A

A B A C D C A B A
(This is really: **ABA   CDC   ABA**)
                              A   **B**   **A**

Multimovement Forms

movement

The importance of form to create cohesiveness in a musical composition extends itself to works with several complete movements. A **movement** is a complete composition that can stand alone, but which forms part of a larger musical work. If a building were considered, each wing has its own purpose

149

and design, but together the entire structure is visible and perceived as a whole.

In multimovement works such as the dance suite, sonata, string quartet, concerto, and symphony, common motivic and melodic material may carry from one movement to the next. But, generally the unifying elements are the tonal center and, as diagrammed below, the tempo of each movement.

Dance Suite   Six dances: Slow—Fast—Slow—Fast—Slow—Fast

Concerto   Three movements: Fast—Slow—Fast

Sonata
String quartet   Four movements: Fast—Slow—Minuet—Fast
Symphony   (The minuet eventually became a *scherzo*.)

Listening Composition

THE RITE OF SPRING: *Ritual of Abduction*
Contemporary Style Period

IGOR STRAVINSKY
1882-1971

Born near Saint Petersburg, Russia, Igor Stravinsky was the son of a famous bass singer at the Imperial Opera. The young Stravinsky was provided with piano lessons, and his father's musical background exposed him to many opera and ballet performances. Even with this early introduction and encouragement, he showed little inclination to pursue a musical career. Then, when he was a law student, he began to study musical technique and composition with Nikolai Rimsky-Korsakov.

Perhaps one of the most important occasions of Stravinsky's life was when he met the director of the Russian Ballet, Sergei Diaghilev, in 1909 in Paris. Stravinsky composed three ballets specifically for the dance company, and these ballets catapulted him into the musical limelight. The first, The Firebird, established him as a major composer. The second, Petrushka, also captivated its audiences in Paris. But the third, The Rite of Spring, led its first Parisian audience to riot in outrage at the "barbarity" of its sounds. The primitive burlap costumes of the dancers, along with the harsh dissonances and striking orchestral effects, shocked many in the audience. Some were shouting, "He is crazy! He is crazy," while others proclaimed, "Genius!" One person is reported to have said, "Quiet, quiet! Listen to the music, then boo!" A humiliated Stravinsky left the theater before the performance was over. Today, The Rite of Spring is revered as a masterpiece and remains one of the most influential pieces of 20th century music.

When World War I began, Stravinsky fled to Switzerland. He lived there until 1920, when he moved to France. Then in 1939, he moved to the United States, becoming a citizen in 1945. He settled in California, and spent the remainder of his life lecturing, conducting, writing, touring the world as a pianist, and writing musical scores for the film industry.

Stravinsky was a clever businessman. He had no use for the "starving genius" image of a composer. He made sure he was well-paid for his work. At one point, he was offered $4,000 to compose the music for a film. He refused, saying it was not enough money. The producer told Stravinsky that another famous composer had recently accepted that amount for a film. Stravinsky retorted, "He has talent. I have not, so for me the work is more difficult."

In 1942, Stravinsky composed his Circus Polka for the Ringling Brothers, Barnum and Bailey Circus. Choreographer George Balanchine had been asked to arrange a ballet for the elephants, and he called Stravinsky, asking him to compose some music. Stravinsky, not knowing the full story, asked what kind of music. Balanchine told him, "A polka." "For whom?" was the next question. "Elephants," came the reply. "How old?" Stravinsky asked. "Young!" said Balanchine. Stravinsky answered, "Okay, if they are very young, I'll do it." That ballet was performed at least 425 times. Perhaps this is what led Stravinsky to quip in 1961, "My music is best understood by children and animals."

Stravinsky was highly respected in all circles for his integrity. As with his musical compositions, in all areas of life he was confident and self-assured. Raised in the Russian Orthodox church, Stravinsky rejected that faith while in his teens. But, almost thirty years later, he converted back to Christianity. In his book "Poetics of Music," Stravinsky states, "Music comes to reveal itself as a form of communion with our fellow man — and with the Supreme Being.

Stravinsky had rethought melody, harmony, orchestration, and rhythm. And although his musical style has many distinguishing traits, it was in constant flux. Like his friend Pablo Picasso, Stravinsky continually searched for new ways to express himself, and explored unknown realms. He was fascinated with the rhythms and other characteristics of ragtime and jazz. He explored nearly every musical idea of the 20th century. Ironically, it was this constant search that led Igor Stravinsky to what inspired him the most, applying old techniques to his modern ideas. The influence of Igor Stravinsky's music has been universal among composers of this century.

Representative Composition

THE RITE OF SPRING: *Ritual of Abduction*

Type of Composition: **Movement from a Ballet**

Overview: Stravinsky states that the inspiration to write this composition was a dream in which he had a vision of a pagan Russian rite, with elders seated in a circle, watching a young girl dance herself to death. Her sacrifice was to appease the god of spring. He had described the dream as "Freudian," and it may have been because five years before this composition was begun, Stravinsky had set to music poems by Sergei Gorodetsky. In that book is found a description of celebrations to Yarila, the god of Spring. Part of the poem is:

At the fore, shaggy, lean, hoar of head,
Moves the wizard, as old as his runes;
He has lived over two thousand moons,
And the axe he inhumed.
On the far lakes he loomed
Long ago,
It is his: the first blow
At the trunk.

And two priestesses in their tenth Spring
To the old one they bring.
In their eyes
Terror lies.
Like the trunk their young bodies are bright.
Their wan white
Has she only, the tender young linden.

One he took, one he led,
To the trunk roughly wed,
A white bride.
And the axe rose and hissed—
And a voice was upraised
And then died.
Thus the first blow was dealt to the trunk.

About the early twentieth century in Russia, it was written that "mystical anarchism was in the air." There was belief in the possibility of a new mythological age—the belief that the vital forces of man's elemental nature were to burst the fetters of civilization and world order.

Structure: **Continuous Form**. A true reflection of what has been called "the prime example of Primitivism," this scene from the ballet presents spontaneous fragments and "splatterings" of melody and harmony. The emphasis is on chaotic activity, asymmetrical melodic figures, irregular rhythms, and dissonant chords.

TIME	COMMENTARY
0:00	A dissonant chord is sustained while accented beats are struck by the timpani as conflicting and overlapping melodic fragments are stated. The feeling is one of chaos.
0:13	"Horn calls," using naturally occurring intervals in the overtone series, are introduced. The frantic action mixes the horn sounds with melodic figures played by strings, woodwinds and trombones.
0:33	The brass instruments enter with the first clearly-defined melodic motive.
0:41	The horn calls return.
0:47	A reflection of the melodic motive tries to restate itself, but is interrupted by the trombone section playing two disjunct pitches.
0:52	Another reflection of the melodic motive is restated. Chaos continues with irregular rhythmic accents until the music comes to a close with a sudden drop to a pianissimo dynamic level and trills by the flutes.

Chapter 12
THE EXPANSION OF IDEAS

The changes in every aspect of life between the period of the Renaissance and the present can be summarized with words such as experimentation, accumulation of information, specialization, and diversity. Reflect upon changes that have occurred in medicine, transportation, politics, philosophy, technology, etc. Music has not been an exception. The development of music has been a continuous expansion of ideas.

VOCAL MUSIC

Opera

An experiment by a small group of poets, artists, musicians, and philosophers in Florence, Italy led to changes of astounding proportions in vocal and, eventually, instrumental music. This group, known as the Florentine Camerata, having an interest in the songs, dances, and drama of the ancient Greeks, came to the conclusion that in Greek theater the lines of the characters were sung, not spoken. The Camerata set out to write and produce such a play. This led to the presen-

opera

tation of the first **opera** — a staged dramatic work utilizing acting, costumes, make up, and scenery in which all lines of the characters are sung.

The most revolutionary result of the opera experiment came about because of the need for characters to present individual lines of dialogue. This presented a problem to composers who had been trained in the writing of the complex polyphony of the Renaissance. The solution for them was a new homophonic style in which a single melody was accompanied by only a bass part and an improvised chordal part. This new manner of melodic presentation was called **monody**. Since the chords were improvised it was only necessary for the composer to write two lines of music, the melody and the bass. The composer did, however, use numbers placed below the bass part to indicate which chord was to be used. The person playing the chords relied on this **figured bass**, but freely delivered the indicated chord in any rhythmical fashion desired, along with trills, turns, and connecting scale passages. Thus, each performance of a song was somewhat different.

monody

figured bass

The instruments typically used to play the chords were lute, harp, harpsichord, and organ. The bass line could be carried by the viola da gamba (about the same size as a cello), bassoon, trombone, or the low pitches of the organ. The combination of bass instrument and chord instrument was known as the **basso continuo**.

basso continuo

Opera rapidly became popular among all classes of people. Sung in the vernacular, familiar stories were told and retold. It was common for entire families to attend, even bringing lunches and snacks to the performance. Great singers were given the most enthusiastic praise, while those less admirable would receive boos and jeers — and maybe even a showering of tomatoes, lettuce, and fruit thrown from the far corners of the theater.

Musically, opera consists of the following components:

Overture   Instrumental introduction. Often presents melodic themes or moods of the story to follow.

	Sometimes is a complete multimovement work in itself.
Ritornello	Short instrumental fillers played during move-ment on stage or between verses of an aria.
Sinfonia	Instrumental interlude played between scenes. Also, confusingly, the term has been used at times in place of both the terms *overture* and *ritornello*.
Chorus	A group of singers. The chorus may be formed by combining the voices of the staged cast members, or, especially in early opera, may be a separate body, independent of the action on stage.
Recitative	A composition and singing style developed for the purpose of moving through the dialogue portion of the story. Of limited pitch range and following natural speech inflections, it is usu-ally fast-paced and rhythmically free. Often presented with minimumal accompaniment.
Aria	An elaborate, self-contained song for solo voice. Usually with full instrumental accompani-ment, an *aria* allows a singer to demonstrate agility and power. Sung in a style called **bel canto**, which literally means *beautiful singing*, an aria will often exhibit an extended pitch range, trills, rapid scales, and other vocal gym-nastics.

bel canto

The above elements were carried into church presentations. An opera based on a sacred or biblical theme is called an **oratorio**. A short oratorio is a **cantata**. Oratorios and canta-tas are often performed in a concert setting without costumes and staging.

**oratorio
cantata**

Art Song

art song

The use of the human voice as a trained expressive musical instrument (instead of merely a conveyer of words) led to the development of other musical works. The nineteenth century **art song** is a composition of high artistic and literary quality for voice and piano, giving equal importance to both parts. More than an accompaniment, the piano part will paint pictures of the song's images of love, nature, life, death, etc. as the voice sings the words. Art songs are often presented in **song cycles** which carry a common theme or story.

song cycles

INSTRUMENTAL MUSIC

Trio Sonata

trio sonata

In instrumental music, the old polyphonic style of writing was maintained and brought to its height during the Baroque period. Simultaneously, the influence of monody in opera was reflected in a new development: The combination of two melody instruments of equal importance, playing in the old polyphonic style and supported by a basso continuo, form the basis for a type of composition known a **trio sonata**. Remembering that the *basso continuo* consists of a bass instrument and a chord instrument, how can *four* players be called a *trio* — two melody instruments + bass + chords? Because, the composer only wrote three parts. As with the basso continuo of monody, the chordal part was improvised by the performer.

dance suite
sonata de camera
sonata de chiesa

The trio sonata was commonly presented as a group of dances called a **dance suite**. If a suite were to be performed in a private home, it was called a **sonata de camera**, a chamber sonata. But, the dance music could be given different titles and used in church, resulting in the name **sonata de chiesa**, a church sonata.

Concerto Grosso

The trio sonata allowed for the development of high skill levels on the part of the individual players. This attention reciprocally brought greater attention to instrumental music and to an interest in orchestras of greater size. Composers writing for larger numbers of performers developed the **concerto grosso**, a multimovement work contrasting the virtuosity of a small group (essentially a trio sonata) with a more forceful large group. The small group, known as the **concertino**, alternated with the large group, the **ripieno**. Each return to the ripieno generally presented the same recognizable theme, resulting in the name **ritornello** (*return*) **form**. The concertino and ripieno playing together comprise the **tutti**. The movements of a concerto grosso typically were three in number and were arranged fast-slow-fast.

The present-day **solo concerto** is a reflection of the concerto grosso. The fast-slow-fast order of the movements is maintained, as is the large group sound contrasting the virtuoso abilities of, in this case, a lone soloist.

Symphony

As the concerto grosso continued, less of a distinction was made between concertino and ripieno. Eventually, the entire ensemble was considered as a whole, a **symphony**, literally meaning *sounding together*. Traces of the contrasting groups are clearly heard in the **sonata form** of the Classical period symphony. As can be seen in the diagram below, sonata form maintains the Baroque preference for binary form, but gives way to the Classical desire for a return to the ideas stated at the beginning — ternary form.

In the **exposition** two contrasting themes — or, more accurately, *theme groups*, related by key center — and a closing theme are presented. Then, in the **development** the com-

concerto grosso

concertino
ripieno

ritornello form
tutti

solo concerto

symphony

sonata form

exposition

development

161

SONATA FORM

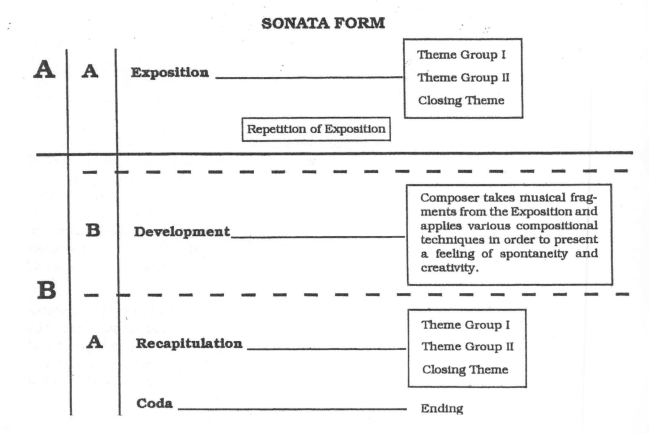

poser is given freedom to work with any previously stated thematic material — almost like improvisation. Finally, in the **recapitulation** the opening themes and theme groups are restated. An ending, the **coda** — literally a *tail* — concludes the music.

recapitulation
coda

The Role of Instruments

Appropriate to the Classical period, the sonata form became predictable, as did the roles of the instruments in the orchestra. The strings were the leaders, playing the main melodies and counter melodies. The woodwinds would sometimes double a melody or add harmonic support. The role of the brass and percussion was to add emphasis to loud passages. With the emerging of Romanticism came a larger orchestra — more instruments and extended families of instruments — and roles of equal importance among the instruments.

piano

One instrument, the **piano**, became the dominant musical instrument of the nineteenth and twentieth centuries. The harpsichord of the Baroque and early Classical period, with its soft sound and inability to execute crescendos and decrescendos, could not keep up with the Romantic spirit. Even the harpsichord's role as the chord provider in the trio sonata was taken over by the viola in what became a favorite of composers, the string quartet.

The piano, invented in 1710 in Italy, was brought into prominence by German musicians. The instrument presently has a pitch range wider than that of a symphony orchestra and has the ability to play lyrical passages, very light and fast runs, dark brooding expressions, and bright and brilliant fortissimos.

Major Trends

The Romantic spirit stretched all music concepts to the limit. And, this same spirit extends to music of today. Symmetrical phrases of predictable length gave way to asymmetrical of any proportions. Tempo, meter, and dynamics took on the ability to change drastically from one note to the next. Melodies could be either long and elaborately interwoven or short and fragmented. Harmony, once firmly grounded on basic structures and formulated progressions, submitted to chords of intentional vagueness and introspection. Reacting to the theories of Charles Darwin, Frederick Nietzsche, Karl Marx, and Sigmund Freud, the music of the late nineteenth and early twentieth centuries reflects the composers' internal struggles, questions of identity, and even the meaning of life itself. The resulting developments were **nationalism**, **impressionism**, **primitivism**, **expressionism**, and **neoclassicism**.

nationalism

Nationalism.   **Nationalism** in music could be defined as music derived from a composer's conscious efforts to draw attention to distinctive elements of a particular country or region, especially drawing from the resources of folk songs and dances. But, the nationalism of the late 1800's was much deeper than that. Spurred by Darwin's concepts of *survival of the strongest*, and — by logical continuation — Nietzsche's *superhuman race*, composer and essayist Richard Wagner in Germany purported the superiority of the Teutonic people. Composers in surrounding areas rebelled against this idea and focused attention on the traditional music and legends of their particular countries in order to free themselves of foreign associations.

Impressionism.   Associated in many ways with nationalism, a movement against the German tendency to promote philosophy through the arts occurred in Paris, France. This movement attempted to address human experience by means of extreme subjectivity, vagueness, and understatement. Poets, painters, sculptors, and musicians sought to present the world, not as a realistic reflection, but as a series of moods and hazy images. In the visual arts and in music this was

impressionism

called **impressionism**. Impressionists, unlike German artists, not only avoided giving answers to the serious questions of life, but even escaped reality altogether. The harshness and dirtiness of big city life in Paris at that time were avoided by means of poems, paintings, and music about nature, boats on a lake, love in the park, the whimsical antics of mythological creatures in a primordial world, etc.

Primitivism. Inspired by fanciful images of a barbaric and uncivilized prehistory, artists and musicians at the turn of the twentieth century translated these suggestions into pictures and sound. In a style called **primitivism**, artists such as Picasso attempted to convey childlike (primitive man) techniques through crude painting and superimposed geometric figures, while composers created scenes of pagan rituals and human sacrifice by means of savage rhythms, angular melodies, and elemental harmony.

Expressionism. In the early part of this century attention was once again turned to Vienna, Austria, the city of Haydn, Mozart, Beethoven, Schubert, and many other famous musicians. But, the strong attraction, at first, was not to the arts but to Sigmund Freud, the psychoanalyst. Freud delved into the world of the unconscious, the world of dreams, distortions of reality, hauntings of childhood events, and unspeakable desires. These visions of the subconscious mind were then depicted in the visual and performing arts under the name **expressionism**. Painters would either draw grotesque and dreamlike exaggerations of people in misery (images attractive to those purporting Marxist communism at the time) or splatter paint onto canvas in any form and manner in order to *express* their subconscious feelings. Similarly, composers set dreamlike lyrics to music, created erose melodies, and presented *splatterings* of disjointed rhythmic fragments. Since the founding of music on a key center creates focus and stability, tonality was declared *passe*, and the move was made to strictly atonal music. However, avoiding the tendency toward a tonal center was not an easy task. Harmonic dissonance helped blur the main tone, as did the sidestepping of smooth connections between pitches by means of disjunct melodies and irregular rhythms. The final break with tonal music came through a new system of composing called **serialism**. In this system, the twelve pitches of the octave are

primitivism

expressionism

serialism

165

tone row

placed in series called a **tone row**. No single pitch can be repeated until all twelve pitches have been used. This makes all tones equal so that none gains special attention.

Neoclassicism. The late nineteenth and early twentieth centuries had posed many life changing questions, and the arts had attempted to address those questions. But the answers, like the theories that brought about the questions, were based on imagination, feelings, personal subjectivity, and isolation. After the harshness of World War I, artists began to realize how far their thoughts and their works had strayed from communicating with a larger population in a real world. Therefore, a return was made to the models of clarity, restraint, and control established in the 18th century.

neoclassicism

This return was called **neoclassicism**. Dissonance was still used, but in the very exact environment of tonality. Large-scale programmatic compositions based on emotionalism and subjectivity were abandoned for a smaller orchestra and small ensembles performing absolute music. Melody and phrasing were generally clear and symmetrical, the texture was usually transparent, and the compositional forms of the Baroque and Classical periods were utilized.

Current Trends

In the world of art music today, the two main philosophical attitudes of romanticism and classicism continue. Some composers carry on the concepts established by the tone row. The idea of a set formula to determine a series of pitches is extended to rhythm, harmony, texture, and timbre. The ele-

chance music

ment of randomness — **chance music** — can be used to either establish the formulas (using dice or cards, for example), or to eliminate any formula or pattern whatsoever.

When the twelve fundamental pitches of the western music system are found to be confining, pitches in between the

quarter tones

pitches ("in the cracks") called **quarter tones** can be used.

One example places half of an orchestra slightly out of tune with the other half. The proclamation, "All sounds are musical," allows composers to incorporate such devices as the squeaking of a clarinet reed, the mutterings of a trumpet with the valves only half depressed, scraping of a bow below the bridge of a cello, and singing into a flute while playing the keys.

During the 1950's and '60's composers experimented with the manipulation of sounds by means of the tape recorder. The tape of vibrations of any given sound — water dripping, for example — could be sped up or slowed down to any degree, presented backwards, or cut and spliced in any number of ways. Today, composers continue to experiment with sound manipulation, but do so by means of computers and synthesizers. These instruments allow an indefinite variety of pitches and timbres, and preprogrammed music can be played at tempos that are humanly impossible to play. Unfortunately, even with the astounding capabilities of the preprogrammed music, an attempt to perform *on stage* with the computer is a rather dull experience because the preprogramming lacks the spontaneity and warmth of a live performance.

Many of the sounds are very intriguing and, intellectually, the music is exciting. Every serious composer is trying to say something, no matter what the tools, and the academic study of ways and means is stimulating — like solving a puzzle, investigating technology, finding out "Who-dun-it." Also, the instrumental and vocal technical training required to play many twentieth-century compositions has elevated the quality of every style of music. And, the use of synthesizers has provided the composers of large works the capability of doing something never before possible, the capability of hearing the work instantly, at the moment it is written. All instruments, pitches, rhythms, dynamics, etc. can be programmed into the synthesizer.

However, this style of contemporary art music has not received a wide audience when presented in a concert setting. Is this because present-day composers are continuing to do what artists have done throughout history — paint a picture of society in which they live — and the dissonance, atonality, disjunct melodies, and asymmetrical rhythms are too much a reflection of this world's frustration over poverty and hopelessness, pollution, congestion, and personal isolation? Or, is the contemporary artist just ahead of his/her time and the public's ear will eventually catch up? The following statement by August von Kotzebue in 1806 would indicate that this latter premise is a possibility:

> The Overture to Beethoven's opera FIDELIO was performed recently, and all impartial musicians and music lovers were in complete agreement that never was anything written in music so incoherent, shrill, muddled, and utterly shocking to the ear.

These questions and others remain, but some contemporary composers take a more conservative approach than the ones mentioned previously. They are continuing to look at new sources — music and instruments of non-western cultures, the sounds of nature, patterns in music based on patterns observed in crystals and molecules, etc. — but are focusing on an integration of tried and tested compositional methods of the past. These composers strive to touch the emotional side of their audiences more than the intellectual side. When criticized for failing to be leaders into the future, they reply that the world must be tended to and healed *today* in order for there to be a future.

Listening Composition

PIERROT LUNAIRE: *Moondrunk*
Contemporary Style Period

ARNOLD SCHOENBERG
1874-1951

Vienna-born Arnold Schoenberg is considered one of the greatest musical innovators of the 20th century. At the age of 8, he began learning the violin, and at 9 he began composing — without formal instruction. Most of Schoenberg's vast knowledge of music came from playing in amateur groups, studying scores, and going to concerts. He was almost entirely self-taught.

Schoenberg supported himself by working as a bank clerk until he was 21. When he lost this job, he decided to devote himself entirely to music. Working in both Berlin and Vienna, Schoenberg orchestrated operettas and conducted a cabaret orchestra, but not with great success. Most of his own compositions were greeted with hostility at their premieres. In 1904, he began to teach composition and music theory in Vienna.

Considered by some to be revolutionary, Schoenberg's innovative techniques began to surface in 1909. Abandoning the traditional tonal system, he wrote a piano piece, Opus 11, No. 1, which is the first "atonal" composition. (It should be noted that Schoenberg disliked the term atonal, or nontonal, because it describes only what the music is not, instead of what the music is. He preferred the term "pantonal" because it indicates that the music includes all tones.) Possessed by his innovation, Schoenberg said, "I have a mission. I am but the loudspeaker of an idea." Schoenberg gained worldwide attention with these atonal works.

In 1910, Schoenberg was still trying to make ends meet. He sent a letter to his publisher asking for work of any kind — "proofreading, piano arrangements, or the like." Having only a few pupils that year, he needed to supplement his income. He wrote:

> *My income has shrunk, and my expenses have increased. So I must do something... . You know that I paint. What you do not know is that my work is highly praised by experts. What I have in mind is that you might be able to get one or the other well-known patron to buy some of my pictures or have his portrait done by me. Only you must not tell people that they will like my pictures. You must make them realize that they have to like my pictures, because they have been praised by authorities on painting; and above all it is much more interesting to have one's portrait done by or to own a painting by a musician of my reputation than to be painted by some mere practitioner of painting whose name will be forgotten in 20 years, whereas even now my name belongs to the history of music. But there is just one thing: I cannot*

consider letting the purchase of a portrait depend on whether the sitter likes it or not. The sitter knows who is painting him; he must also realize that he understands nothing about such things, but that the portrait has artistic value, or, to say the least of it, historical value.

In 1912, he wrote *Pierrot Lunaire*, a song cycle of 21 German poems. With this piece, Schoenberg introduced the technique of Sprechstimme, or "speech voice," where the lyrics are half-spoken, half-sung. Then in 1921, Schoenberg revealed a concept which would change music forever. He told a student, "I have made a discovery which will ensure the supremacy of German music for the next hundred years." Within two years, he began publishing compositions using his new twelve-tone system. His music gained the respect of many important musicians, though it was not accepted by the larger audience.

It is rather unlikely that Schoenberg was fazed by whether his music was accepted. When told that a particular violin concerto was so difficult to play, it required a soloist with six fingers, Schoenberg retorted, "Very well, I can wait." During a more serious moment, Schoenberg reflecting on himself stated, "I want to be seen as above personalities. I want to be seen as one who is expressing in music the desire of the human soul in its search for God."

Representative Composition

PIERROT LUNAIRE: *Moondrunk*

Type of Composition: **Part of a Song Cycle**

Overview: This composition is the first of a cycle of twenty-one songs using poems of the same name by a surrealist, Albert Giraud. Pierrot is a lunatic clown (the singer is in costume during performance), representing the expressionist artist of the early twentieth century in the search to find the distinction between fantasy and reality. A clearer image of the dream-like, subconscious nature of the poems might be seen in poem number 16:

Into the bald head of Cassender,
Whose screams rend the air,
Pierrot bores, pretending to be sweet,
Using a skull drill.

Then he stuffs with his thumb,
His own genuine Turkish tobacco
Into the bald head of Cassender,
Whose screams rend the air.

Then he inserts the stem of his pipe,
Deep into the smooth, bald head
And comfortably draws and puffs,
His own genuine Turkish tobacco,
Into the bald head of Cassender.

In the twenty-one musical settings, the speaker/singer is accompanied by ensembles using combinations of piano, flute, clarinet, bass clarinet, violin, viola, and cello. Musicologist Philip Friedheim states, "The continual use of the vocal glissando, which encompasses pitches that lie outside the well-tempered scales of Western music, accompanied by instruments that also exploit unusual sonorities (piano harmonics, extreme ranges, pizzicato glissandos in the strings, flutter-tonguing in the winds, etc.), creates a highly unstable texture that covers an emotional gamut from morbid depression to pathological hysteria."

Structure: **Continuous Form**. As dreams are surreal and without structure, so, generally, are the works of Expressionist artists (although Schoenberg does use the canon form for numbers 17 and 18 of this cycle, and the recurring lines in the poems create definition). This is the case in the musical setting of the first poem of Pierrot Lunaire. The voice seems unreal, using Schoenberg's newly-invented technique of Sprechstimme in which the text is half-spoken and half-sung.

TIME	GERMAN	ENGLISH
0:00	Den Wein, den man mit Augen trinkt, Giesst nachts der Mond in Wogen nieder, Und eine Springflut überschwemmt Den stillen Horizont.	The wine that one drinks with the eyes, Pours at night from the moon in waves, And a springflood overflows The still horizon.

0:38	Gelüste, schauerlich and süss, Durchschwimmen ohne Zahl die Fluten! Den Wein, den man mit Augen trinkt, Giesst nachts der Mond in Wogen nieder.	Desires, shivering and sweet, Swim without number through the flood, The wine that one drinks with the eyes, Pours at night from the moon in waves.
1:02	Der Dichter, den die Andacht triebt, Berauscht sich an dem heilgen Tranke, Den Himmel wendet er verzückt das Haupt Und taumelnd saugt und schlürft er Den Wein, den man mit Augen trinkt.	The poet, by ardor driven, Enraptured with the holy drink, To heaven he joyfully lifts his head, And reeling, sips and slurps, The wine that one drinks with the eyes.

APPENDIX
NOTATED MUSIC EXAMPLES

Alleluia

Angels We Have Heard On High

Are You Sleeping

Camptown Races

Home on the Range

I've Been Working On the Railroad

Jingle Bells

Joy To the World, the Lord Is Come

Mary Had a Little Lamb

Mickey Mouse Club Song

My Country, 'Tis of Thee

Pop Goes the Weasel

Red River Valley

Row, Row, Row Your Boat

Somewhere Over the Rainbow

The Star Spangled Banner

Swing Low, Sweet Chariot

This Old Man

This Train

When the Saints Go Marching In

Yankee Doodle

Alleluia
(examples)

Angels We Have Heard on High

177

Are You Sleeping

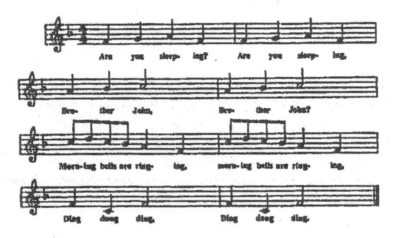

Camptown Races

Home On the Range

I've Been Working On the Railroad

181

Mary Had A Little Lamb

My Country, 'Tis of Thee

182

183

The Star Spangled Banner

184

Swing Low, Sweet Chariot

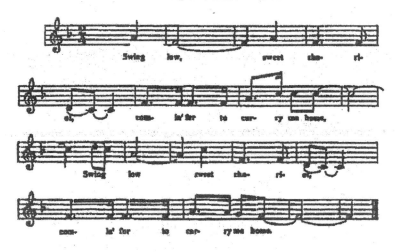

This Old Man

This Train

When The Saints Go Marching In

Yankee Doodle

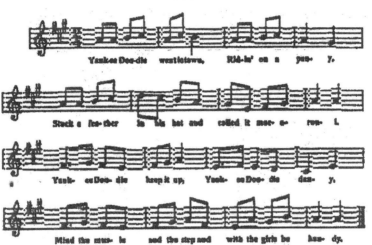

Yan-kee Doo-dle went to town, Rid-in' on a pon-y.

Stuck a fea-ther in his hat and called it mac-a-ro-ni.

Yank-ee Doo-dle keep it up, Yank-ee Doo-dle dan-dy.

Mind the mus-ic and the step and with the girls be han-dy.

GLOSSARY

absolute music   Music that conveys emotion and meaning without the need for words or images.

accelerando   Gradually speeding up.

accent   Giving special emphasis or attention to a sound.

additive form   The type of sectional musical form in which new music sections are added to existing sections.

aerophones   Instruments whose sound is produced when *air* in an enclosed chamber is set into motion.

analytical listener   Someone who listens for the details of rhythm, melody, harmony, instrumental technique, and historical performance practices.

aperture   A hole in an air column over which air is passed in order to disturb the air inside the column.

aria   Part of opera, an elaborate song used to show off the human voice.

art song   A composition of high artistic and literary quality for voice and piano.

articulation   The manner in which pitches are started, sustained, and stopped.

associative listener   Someone who uses music as it relates to other activities.

atonal music   Music that lacks a tonal center (see Tonal Music).

augmentation	Making the durations of the pitches of a motive or melody longer.
basso cantante	A lighter and smoother low male voice.
basso continuo	The Baroque conbination of a bass instrument and a chord instrument.
basso profundo	A very low powerful male voice.
bel canto	A style of singing requiring training and mastery of vocal techniques.
binary form	A two-part form outlined as sections **A B**.
boy soprano	A young male singing in a high pitch range.
brass instruments	Instruments of the trumpet, trombone, French horn, and tuba families.
cadence	A pause or resting place.
cambiato	An adolescent male singer at the age when the voice is changing.
canon	A polyphonic composition, based on strict imitation, in which a melody in one part is followed at a short distance by the same melody in another part, so that the melody overlaps itself.
canonic technique	A method of composition in which the initial impression is one of strict imitation, as if a canon were beginning, but then the parts move into more freely composed polyphony.
cantata	A short oratorio.
castrato	A man who, during youth, had had his testicles removed in order to prevent the voice from changing.
chordophones	Instruments whose sounds are produced by vibrating strings.
chorus	A group of singers.

classical	Following a prescribed model for achieving success, objectivity, fixed routines, clarity of formal design, balance, formulas, status quo, simplicity, and craftsmanship.
coloratura	Refers to a soprano with an extremely high range and the ability to exhibit such virtuoso techniques as rapid scale passages, trills, and wide leaps.
concerto grosso	A multimovement work contrasting a small group with a large group.
conjunct movement	Melodic movement in which a pitch moves to a nearby pitch.
consonant harmony (consonance)	Harmony with a sensation of stability and the absence of tension.
continuous form	Compositions which cannot be broken into separate independent bodies, meaning that the music begins and continues with only new material until the end.
contrasting phrases	Two phrases which start differently.
countertenor	A man who has practiced making his high *falsetto* voice (in the women's range) strong and controlled.
chord	The simultaneous sounding of three or more pitches.
cps	Cycles per second. Used synonymously with *vps* and *hz*.
crescendo	Gradually moving from one dynamic level to a louder level.
dance suite	A group of dances.
decibels	The term used to scientifically measure dynamics (abbreviated *db*).
decrescendo	Gradually getting softer.
diminution	Making the duration of the pitches of a motive or melody shorter.
disjunct movement	Melodic movement in which a pitch skips others in order to arrive at a second pitch.

dissonant harmony (dissonance)   Harmony with the feeling of instability and tension. Dissonance is often described as a clashing of pitches.

dramatic soprano   A woman with a powerful voice who will sing music which utilizes the lower pitch spectrum of her range.

duration   The length of time the tone exists.

dynamic level (dynamics)   The music term which refers to loudness and softness.

electrophones   Instruments whose sounds are created through electronic means.

embouchure   Placement and pressure of the mouth and lips on an instrument.

enigmatic music   The general name for musical mysteries and puzzles.

fermata   Holding a sound for an indeterminate length of time.

figured bass   Numbers placed beneath the bass part of a composition to indicate which chords are to be played.

form   The elements of cohesion and structure in music.

frequency   The rate of speed of the vibrations of a given pitch.

functional harmony   Harmony with a utilitarian purpose.

grace note   A pitch that is very briefly sounded, quickly moving to a nearby emphasized pitch.

Gregorian chant   The songs of the Christian church, compiled and cataloged by Pope Gregory (540-609A.D.) at the beginning of the 7th century.

harmony   The simultaneous sounding of two or more pitches.

heroic   A descriptive term for a powerful dramatic male tenor voice.

homophony   The presentation of a melody with added harmony or harmonic accompaniment.

hz	See *vps*.
idiophone	An instrument in which the sound is produced by the instrument itself vibrating.
imitation	A musical statement that identifiably resembles a previously heard statement.
inversion	Presenting a motive or melody upside down.
jongleurs	Poor itinerant entertainers of the Middle Ages.
keynote (keytone)	In tonal music, the pitch that creates the feeling of completion or finality.
legato	Articulation in which the pitches are smoothly connected together.
lyre	A simple harp-like instrument consisting of a frame on which strings are stretched.
lyric voice	A voice with have a lighter quality, usually describing a soprano or tenor voice.
madrigal	A short lyric poem set to music, usually polyphonic for three to eight voices.
melismatic organum	Polyphony created by a melismatic part heard simultaneously with a Gregorian chant.
Melismatic	A method utilizing many pitches per syllable when adding music to words.
melody	A succession of different pitches of varying durations perceived as an entity.
membranophones	Instruments whose sounds are produced by a tightly stretched *membrane*.
meter	The grouping of beats into regular, recurring patterns.
minnesingers	See *troubadours*.

minstrels	See *jongleurs*.
monody	The Baroque compositional technique of presenting a song with *basso continuo* accompaniment.
monophony (monophonic texture)	A single melody without harmonic support or accompaniment.
motive	The shortest possible complete melodic statement.
movement	1) A complete composition that can stand alone, but which forms part of a larger musical work. 2) Melodic movement: see *conjunct* and *disjunct movement*.
musical tone	The result of air molecules being displaced by something moving in a smooth consistent pattern.
mute	A device that changes the timbre of the instrument and lowers the dynamic level.
neumatic	A method utilizing two or three pitches per syllable when adding music to words.
Noh dramas	Classic Japanese court drama, with music and dance, based on philosophical and heroic subject matter.
noise	The result of irregular vibrations being produced.
opera	A staged dramatic work in which all lines of the characters are sung.
oratorio	An opera based on a sacred or biblical theme.
organum	A term referring to the harmony of the Middle Ages.
ornamentation	Musical embellishments, such as *vibrato, trills,* and *grace notes*.
overtones	Sub vibrations produced simultaneously when a musical tone is produced.
overture	Instrumental introduction to an opera or oratorio.

parallel organum   The harmony created when pitches are placed at a fixed distance above a Gregorian chant.

parallel phrases   Two phrases which start the same.

passive listener   Someone who is really not a listener at all but who uses music as a background for other activities.

percussion   Instruments of the membranophone and idiophone families whose sounds are produced by hitting, rubbing, scraping, shaking, or rattling.

phrase   A longer melodic statement, usually ending with a cadence.

pitch   The relative *highness* or *lowness* of sound.

polyphony   The simultaneous sounding of two or more melodies.

program music   Music which tells a story or paints a specific picture.

quarter tone   Any pitch which falls between two adjacent pitches in the Western tonal system.

quodlibet   Two or more well-known songs performed simultaneously.

Ramayana chants   Rhythmic songs of Balinese religious ceremonies which recount the epic stories (originally from India) of the monkey god, Ramayana.

recitative   A compositional style used in opera for moving through the dialogue portions of the story.

reed   A thin piece of bamboo used on various woodwind instruments. Causing the reed to vibrate causes the air in the instrument to vibrate.

repetition   The resounding of a musical statement.

retrograde   Writing a motive or melody backwards.

return forms   Sectional forms which repeat previously heard sections.

rhythm	The movement or driving force in music. A term referring to all time aspects of music.
ritardando	Gradually slowing down.
ritornello	A short instrumental filler used in opera.
ritornello form	In a concerto grosso, the practice of periodically returning to a main melody.
romantic	Breaking away from set models, subjectivity, imagination, sensuality, exploration, and challenging the status quo.
round	See *canon*.
rubato	The alternation between slight amounts of speeding up and slowing within a composition.
sectional form	A musical composition that can be broken down into larger well-defined units of material.
sequence	An orderly and predictable imitation of a melodic motive.
simple song form form	A small structural unit, usually consisting two parallel phrases.
sonata form	Commonly used form for movements of sonatas, symphonies, and concertos. Consists of three parts: the exposition in which the themes are developed, the development in which the material of the exposition is expanded upon, and the recapitulation in which there is a clear return to the themes.
sinfonia	An instrumental interlude played between the scenes of an opera.
sonata	A multi-movement composition for a solo instrument, or for an instrument with piano accompaniment.
song cycle	A group of art songs with a common theme or story.
songs of geste	Poems of courtly love, the beauty or hostility of nature, and knightly heroic deeds set to music.

sopranist A countertenor who specializes in singing the high parts of Middle Ages and Renaissance music.

soundboard Light, flexible wood connected to the strings of a chordophone, used to produce a louder sound.

staccato Articulation in which the pitches are short and detached.

strophic The type of sectional musical form in which a song is repeated, over and over again.

style The identifiable characteristics of how an individual or many individuals employ the other elements of music.

syllabic A method utilizing only one pitch per syllable when adding music to words.

symphony A multimovement work for orchestra.

syncopation The placing of stress on a beat or part of a beat that is normally not emphasized.

tempo A composition's relative rate of speed.

ternary form A return form outlined as sections **A B A.**

terraced dynamics Changes of dynamics by means of sudden shifts from one level to another.

texture The interweaving of melody, melody with harmony, and melody with melody.

theme with variations A type of additive form of musical composition in which a song is repeated over and over but with changes to either melody, harmony, or rhythm with each repetition.

through composed See *continuous form*.

timbre Tone color or tone quality.

tonal music Music in which there is a tonal center, i.e., a particular pitch used to create a feeling of completion or finality.

trill	The rapid alternation between two nearby pitches.
trinary form	A three-part form outlined as sections **A B C**.
trio sonata	Baroque composition consisting of two soloists and basso continuo.
troubadours	Musicians and poets of nobility in southern France in the 12th and 13th centuries with counterparts in northern France, the *trouveres*, and in Germany, the *minnesingers*.
trouveres	See *troubadours*.
vibrato	The slight wavering of a pitch.
vps or hz	Vibrations per second.
word painting	The use of musical elements to describe or paint a picture of the text of a song.

INDEX

Made in the USA
Lexington, KY
30 August 2017